Using Fables with Children

Linda K. Garrity

Illustrated by Jackie Moore

GoodYearBooks

An Imprint of ScottForesman
A Division of HarperCollins*Publishers*

Good Year Books
are available for preschool through grade 6 and for every basic curriculum subject plus many enrichment areas. For more Good Year Books, contact your local bookseller or educational dealer. For a complete catalog with information about other Good Year Books, please write:

Good Year Books
Scott, Foresman and Company
1900 East Lake Avenue
Glenview, Illinois 60025

7 8 9 MAL 99 98 97

Copyright © 1991 Linda K. Garrity.
All Rights Reserved.
Printed in the United States of America.

ISBN 0-673-46317-6

Only portions of this book intended for classroom use may be reproduced without permission in writing from the publisher.

GoodYearBooks
An Imprint of ScottForesman
A Division of HarperCollins*Publishers*

Table of Contents

Introduction 1
Concepts, Teaching Strategies, and Enrichment Activities 3
Activity Pages 13
Fable Texts 37
   The Tortoise and the Hare 39
   The Stag and the Hedgehog 39
   The Crow and the Pitcher 41
   The Lion and the Mouse 41
   The Ant and the Dove 42
   Androcles and the Lion 42
   The Wind and the Sun 43
   The Lion's Share 44
   The Dog and His Shadow 45
   The Goose that Laid the Golden Egg 45
   The Town Mouse and the Country Mouse 46
   The Milkmaid and Her Pail 47
   The Farmer and the Hare 47
   The Dog in the Manger 48
   The Fox and the Stork 48
   The Fox and the Sick Lion 49
   The Lion, the Wolf, and the Fox 49
   The Bundle of Sticks 50
   The Two Travellers and a Bear 51
   The Fox and the Grapes 51
   A Wolf in Sheep's Clothing 52
   The Monkey and the Crocodile 52
   The Boy Who Cried Wolf 53
   The Ant and the Grasshopper 54
   The Hermit and the Mouse 54
   The Donkey in the Lion's Skin 55
   The Hare and the Rumor 56
   The Golden Goose 57
   The Elephant and the Carpenters 58
   The Report Card 59
   The Sneakers 59
   Lunch 60
   The Boy and His Mother 60
Culminating Activity Pages 61
Bibliography 79
Index to Fables 87

Introduction

Today's children enjoy studying fables for the same reason children of ancient times enjoyed them–they are entertaining and thought-provoking. This ancient folklore is an important part of our literary heritage; children need to understand the background and meaning of such expressions as "crying wolf," "sour grapes," or "dog in the manger." As they listen and verbalize the morals of various fables, they also gain proficiency in identifying the main point of a short story, a skill that is critical in comprehending literature. And, as a secondary outcome, children just might achieve the original goal of fables–wisdom about the ways of human beings, told through stories about animals.

Fabulous Fables is a comprehensive study guide for teachers, media specialists, and parents to use with children in second through fourth grade. (Second-graders enjoy fables, though many of them have difficulty with the abstraction of determining morals, especially at the beginning of the unit.) The book provides an organization and background for the unit of study, along with teaching strategies, enrichment activities, versions of the fables, and an annotated bibliography.

Fabulous Fables divides the unit of study into twelve lessons. Each lesson starts with an overview of the concepts or backgrounds of the unit, followed by suggestions for teaching the material. These teaching strategies use specific fables to exemplify each of the concepts. (Each lesson contains page references to the fable texts, which are located in the third section of the book.) The unit of study outlined in *Fabulous Fables* covers most of the major fables of Western civilization and several from Eastern civilization.

The concepts and teaching strategies are followed by a variety of enrichment or extension activities: drama, arts-and-crafts, writing, and research. Many of the activities include references to the reproducible activity pages found in the second section of the book. Since the program can be used with several age groups, there is a range in the enrichment activities; most of the duplicating pages, however, are aimed at the younger children. More complex activities are explained in the text.

The next section features several culminating suggestions–games and activities that require children to possess some knowledge of the fables and proverbs from the unit. Most educators realize that a variety of modes are needed to instruct children; a variety of approaches also makes learning a lot more fun, and that is important too.

Following the culminating activity pages are the fable texts. These have been added for the convenience of the teacher, but they should not preclude use of the many fine books on the market for children today.

The final section contains an annotated bibliography with both individual fables and fable collections. Many of these materials are beautifully illustrated and should be shown, read, or made available for children to read to themselves. With educa-

From *Fabulous Fables: Using Fables with Children*, published by Good Year Books. Copyright © 1991 Linda K. Garrity.

tional dollars so limited these days, the annotated bibliography can be of value to media specialists and teachers trying to build fable collections or even to parents seeking to purchase a few outstanding titles.

Fabulous Fables has been designed to be effective with children and easy for adults to use so that they can pass on a part of their literary folk heritage. The old fables have always been passed on to the new generation with the understanding that they, in turn, will continue the tradition. The discovery and enjoyment of fables, those witty little stories that marvel and mock the ways of humankind, are as enduring as folk wisdom itself.

Concepts, Teaching Strategies, and Enrichment Activities

Concepts, Teaching Strategies, and Enrichment Activites

LESSON CONCEPTS

A. Understanding Morals in Fables
Lesson 1: The Uniqueness of Fables
Lesson 2: Proverbs as Morals
Lesson 3: Fables with Multiple Morals
Lesson 4: Fables with Opposing Morals
Lesson 5: Folk Wisdom in Morals

B. Characteristics of Fables
Lesson 6: The Length of Fables
Lesson 7: Setting
Lesson 8: Animal Characters
Lesson 9: Personification
Lesson 10: Dialogue

C. The History of Fables
Lesson 11: The Origins of Fables
Lesson 12: Modern Fables

LESSON 1 The Uniqueness of Fables

Concepts

1. Fables have remained popular with young and old alike down through the centuries because they contain wisdom and are entertaining.

2. Fables have unique characteristics that set them apart from other forms of literature. In this lesson, we will look at these characteristics:

- Ancient fables are considered folklore because they have been handed down orally and have no single author.

- Fables always teach a lesson, called a moral. The moral is expressed in a concise, complete sentence, and it is usually stated at the end of the fable, set apart by a small space and preceded by the word "Moral:". Sometimes the moral is merely implied, not stated.

Teaching Strategies

If the children in the class are already familiar with fables, ask if they can guess the name of one of the most familiar fables in the Western world. (The fables in Eastern literature will be covered later in the study.) Read aloud "The Tortoise and the Hare," page 39, without reading the moral at the end. Then discuss with the children what they have learned from this story. This discussion can lead into an explanation of a moral, which is a lesson that teaches ethical behavior and attitudes. Children usually start their understanding of morals by first comprehending the theme in their own words and then transferring the meaning to the commonly used proverb.

Now read "The Stag and the Hedgehog," page 39. What do the two fables have in common? How are they different? What different advice do they give on winning races? How would this advice apply to winning or succeeding in real life?

Enrichment Activities

Craft: To accompany "The Tortoise and the Hare," younger children will enjoy making the animals and re-enacting the famous race. See Activity Page 1.

Research: Why is this fable called "The Tortoise and the Hare," rather than "The Rabbit and the Turtle"? What are the differences between tortoises and turtles, and hares and rabbits? Children's encyclopedias contain the information about the animals, which will help children understand that

From *Fabulous Fables: Using Fables with Children,* published by Good Year Books. Copyright © 1991 Linda K. Garrity.

the traditional terms are the better ones for the animals of the story.

Writing: Provide several editions of sports pages from newspapers. After older children have had the opportunity to peruse them, ask them to write sports headlines or even complete sports article parodies for the two racing fables.

Drama: Because of the action involved, these two fables are fun for older children to dramatize for younger children.

Game: Younger children will enjoy making and playing the simple "Tortoise and Hare" race track game, which is made more interesting by using a card deck for advancement. See Activity Page 2.

LESSON 2   Proverbs as Morals

Concepts

Usually, the moral found at the end of a fable is a proverb.

• A proverb is a wise thought, stated very briefly.

• A proverb can be meaningful by itself, but a moral must accompany a text.

• Because proverbs are so brief and easy to remember, they have been used for centuries to teach children and make observations about life's events.

Teaching Strategies

The moral that most adults associate with the fable "The Hare and the Tortoise" is "Slow and steady wins the race." This moral is called a "proverb." It explains the important lesson learned from the story and, used by itself, it is also good advice. The moral to "The Stag and the Hedgehog," "You may need to deal with cheaters by cheating," is not a famous proverb. The difference between morals and proverbs is that all stories have a moral, but only fables have proverbs attached to them.

There are many collections of proverbs that have no fables connected to them at all. On the other hand, some proverbs are so universally associated with a specific fable that it is difficult to think of one without thinking of the other. (This is an abstract concept that you will need to refer to throughout the unit.) Discuss with children the morals or main ideas of current reading material;

it is not so difficult then to see that those main ideas are not in proverb format.

Proverbs are themselves a form of folklore because they have been handed down by word of mouth for generations. Proverbs have been used to teach children proper attitudes and behaviors in earlier times. In fact, children often used to hear the proverb "Children should be seen and not heard." That is an example of both the old-style expectations of children and also of a proverb used without a fable preceding it.

"The Crow and the Pitcher," page 41, is an example of a fable with two equally appropriate proverbs as morals.

Enrichment Activities

Craft: Older children can select a favorite, preferably short, proverb and create a cross stitch sampler using Activity Page 3. (See page 6 for a list of proverbs. Older children may be able to brainstorm some additional ones.) This is a quiet, time-consuming activity that will work well at the end of the day. There is a lot of planning and problem-solving involved. Some older children might want to try their hand at actual cross stitching, but in most cases the paper project will be more appropriate.

Craft: Younger children can practice their alphabetizing skills on this cut-and-paste activity on Activity Page 4.

Research: For examples of proverbs used in children's education, look up *The New England Primer, McGuffey's Eclectic Reader,* and also *Poor Richard's Almanack.*

From *Fabulous Fables: Using Fables with Children,* published by Good Year Books. Copyright © 1991 Linda K. Garrity.

Writing: Proverbs fall into two categories: those that are simple statements, expressing a generally accepted fact; and those that are metaphors or expressions, saying one thing and meaning another. Here are some examples of the two kinds of proverbs. Present them in a mixed order and have children decide which type each proverb is. What are the literal meanings of the metaphorical proverbs?

Simple Statements

Work before play.
Honesty is the best policy.
Seeing is believing.
Waste not, want not.
Try to please everyone and you will please no one.
No one believes a liar.
One good turn deserves another.
He who hesitates is lost.
Practice makes perfect.
Misery loves company.
Silence is golden.
Haste makes waste.
Where there's a will, there's a way.

Metaphors

Don't count your chickens before they hatch.
The grass is always greener on the other side.
Birds of a feather flock together.
When the cat's away, the mice will play.
A watched pot never boils.
The early bird catches the worm.
Too many cooks spoil the broth.
Look before you leap.
One bird in the hand is worth two in the bush
An apple a day keeps the doctor away.
You can lead a horse to water, but you can't make him drink.

Writing: Ask the class to brainstorm old and new proverbs for class rules. Students can then print the proverbs on poster board and display them in the classroom.

LESSON 3
Fables with More Than One Moral

Concepts

Several fables can have the same moral and one fable can have several morals.

- Proverbs were probably developed first, with fables added later to better explain the proverbs.
- Since people are all unique, they may draw different conclusions from the same fable.

Teaching Strategies

Read aloud the following fables, but do not read the morals. Then ask the class what is similar about the fables:
"The Lion and the Mouse," page 41
"The Ant and the Dove," page 42
"Androcles and the Lion," page 42

Discuss the ideas of smaller people and animals being capable of helping larger, more powerful animals and people, and of the value of returning kindnesses or favors. Proverbs often associated with these fables are:

"No act of kindness, no matter how small, ever goes unrewarded."
"One good turn deserves another."
"Small friends can be great friends"
"The small can be mighty."

Which moral fits best with each fable? There is no right or wrong answer, though a slight distinction can be made between inferiors helping superiors as opposed to equals exchanging favors. (An amusing example of irony is the fact that the first proverb "No act of kindness..." is often included in collections of Murphy's Laws.) Emphasize that a moral can be stated in each person's own words, but a proverb is always stated in the exact same form.

From *Fabulous Fables: Using Fables with Children,* published by Good Year Books. Copyright © 1991 Linda K. Garrity.

Enrichment Activities

Writing: The proverbs from this lesson's three fables can be used as a basis for children's writing. In their first attempt at this literary form, it will be easier for children to use people rather than animals for the characters. Older children may prefer to use animal characters, though you should emphasize that each animal should exemplify a particular personality characteristic. Help the group brainstorm examples of things that smaller people (children) can do to help adults. Discuss typical things that adults do to help children. Then discuss favors that equals (either adults or children) do for one another. Write the proverbs on the chalkboard so children can select one, and then write a fable, using that proverb for the moral. (It is wise to suggest that children avoid using classmates' names in the fables.)

Craft: See Activity Page 5 for a maze to accompany "The Lion and the Mouse."

Sequencing: See Activity Page 6, a cut-and-paste sequencing activity to accompany "The Ant and the Dove."

Crossword Puzzle: See Activity Page 7, a crossword puzzle to accompany "Androcles and the Lion."

LESSON 4
Fables with Opposing Morals

Concept

Since cultural values vary, so do the morals of fables. Different fables can teach completely opposite morals.

Teaching Strategies

Read aloud "The Wind and the Sun," page 43, and "The Lion's Share," page 44. Then discuss the following questions with the class: What if you reversed the morals? How would you need to change the fables, so the new morals would work?

Read the following proverb to the class: "You can catch more flies with honey than vinegar." Ask the class the following questions: What does it mean? Which fable would it best match? Here is a proverb that was studied in the previous section: "He who hesitates is lost." Can you think of a proverb that has an opposite meaning? How about "Look before you leap"? Would the fables accompanying these proverbs be similar? Which proverb do you think gives the best advice?

Enrichment Activities

Craft: Different ages will enjoy making the windsocks described on Activity Page 8. Or, students can use different colors and designs to make windsocks for the entire fable collection, with each child choosing a different fable.

Writing or Drama: Children can write or dramatize two short fable skits, exemplifying both of the above-mentioned proverbs.

LESSON 5 Folk Wisdom in Morals

Concept

The folk wisdom found in fables seems to be as appropriate today as it was in ancient times.

Teaching Strategies

One reason fables have been so enduring is that they do not honor the great characteristics of the mighty heroes, but rather the simple down-to-earth wisdom of the common people. Older

From *Fabulous Fables: Using Fables with Children,* published by Good Year Books. Copyright © 1991 Linda K. Garrity.

children might like to discuss whether they think political candidates are elected for their patriotic, heroic traits or for their common sense.

Explain that you will read three fables with similar morals. Write the morals on the board. Then after reading the fables, have the children match the morals to the correct fables.

"The Dog and His Shadow," page 45
"The Goose that Laid the Golden Egg," page 45
"The Town Mouse and the Country Mouse," page 46

What basic idea is similar in all three?

Read aloud "The Milkmaid and Her Pail," page 47, and "The Farmer and the Hare," page 47. The second fable is from Russia and the first one is of unknown European origin. What is similar about the two? What is different? How could they be so similar if they came from different places?

Enrichment Activities

Writing: "The Dog and His Shadow" can trigger a language arts lesson on adjectives in a bulletin board activity for younger children. See Activity Page 9.

Craft: Younger children will enjoy coloring appropriate backgrounds for the two mice from "The Town Mouse and the Country Mouse" on Activity Page 10.

Craft: Children might enjoy making the two mice from halved walnut shells and bits of felt and scraps (similar to the little project that is popular around the holiday season).

Writing: See Activity Page 11 for a sequencing activity to accompany "The Farmer and the Hare."

LESSON 6 The Length of Fables

Concept

Most fables are brief; longer fables, especially those without proverbs stated at the end, are usually classified as folktales.

Teaching Strategies

Some fables are not much longer than a joke. Two examples of short but very well-known fables are: "The Dog in the Manger," page 48, and "The Ant and the Grasshopper," page 54.

"The Goose That Laid the Golden Egg," page 45, is a good example of a fable that can also be classified as a folktale. If possible, show children a version of this folktale from a folktale anthology.

Enrichment Activitiy

Writing: The peasants, when they found the golden egg, immediately thought of material goods that they could buy. Have children use Activity Page 12 to brainstorm either things they could do with riches to help others or things that they value that can't be bought with money.

LESSON 7 Setting

Concepts

1. The storyline of a fable occurs in one or sometimes two scenes.

2. Fables usually have forests and villages as settings.

- The settings show people and animals of long ago.
- The types of animals in the stories indicate the region where the fable was first told.

Teaching Strategies

The fable "The Fox and the Stork," page 48, takes place in two scenes. What is meant by a "scene"?

From *Fabulous Fables: Using Fables with Children,* published by Good Year Books. Copyright © 1991 Linda K. Garrity.

What are the two scenes in this fable?

Read aloud "The Boy Who Cried Wolf," page 53. Then ask the class to think about the setting. Is this a modern-day story? What clues lead them to think that? Would the message apply to today's world? Why or why not? How many scenes are in this fable?

Read "The Monkey and the Crocodile," page 52. In what part of the world was this story first told?

Enrichment Activities

Craft: After hearing "The Fox and the Stork," children will be able to make the three-dimensional craft on Activity Page 13.

Craft: Activity Page 14 offers a delightful pop-up project to accompany "The Monkey and the Crocodile."

LESSON 8   Animal Characters

Concept

Fables usually have animals as main characters. Animals may have been substituted for people in ancient times to avoid offending friends, family, or political leaders.

Teaching Strategies

"The Fox and the Sick Lion," page 49, and "The Lion, the Wolf, and the Fox," page 49, are two fables that start out almost the same, but have different endings and different morals. Ask the class: Since the lion is always called "the king of the jungle or forest," who do you think these fables may have been about?

Two famous fables that have people as main characters are:

"The Bundle of Sticks," page 50
"The Two Travellers and a Bear," page 51

"The Bundle of Sticks" has often been used in political situations. Ask older children to give examples of when the moral of that fable would be appropriate.

Enrichment Activities

Craft: See Activity Page 15 for a pop-up activity to accompany "The Fox and the Sick Lion."

Research: Ask the children to search through newspapers to find editorial or political cartoons that use animals to represent political figures. The donkey and elephant are easiest to find. Discuss what the animals represent.

LESSON 9   Personification

Concept

Each animal character in a fable exemplifies a single characteristic of human personality.

Teaching Strategies

Foxes and wolves are especially prominent characters in fables. Read aloud "The Fox and the Grapes," page 51, and "A Wolf in Sheep's Clothing," page 52. Ask the class the following questions: What main characteristic does each animal possess? Judging from all the fables you've heard, how do foxes and wolves differ? Are these animals actually like they are portrayed in folklore? You may need to read about them to discover their true characteristics.

Brainstorm with the class a list of animals used in fables, and write them on the board. Then write the characteristics most commonly associated with each animal. Ask the class: Is the characteristic always accurate? Judging an entire group by one characteristic is called "stereotyping." Why is it a poor idea to stereotype groups of people (or even groups of animals)?

Enrichment Activity

Writing: Use Activity Page 16 to design job applications for various forest animals.

From *Fabulous Fables: Using Fables with Children*, published by Good Year Books. Copyright © 1991 Linda K. Garrity.

LESSON 10 Dialogue

Concept

Most fables contain dialogue or conversation.

Teaching Strategy

Fable dialogue offers students an opportunity to learn to use quotation marks correctly. This is a difficult skill which requires much practice. After some review of the rules, students can practice using punctuation on copies of any of the fables ("white out" appropriate punctuation before photocopying) or they can do Activity Page 17.

Enrichment Activities

Drama: Dialogue also lends itself to drama. Pairs of students can choose a fable, create simple headwear and act out their favorite fable. They will need to decide on a way of presenting the moral at the end; perhaps a narrator could do this or the characters could recite it in unison. "The Crow and the Pitcher," page 41, is an interesting fable to act out. Students can use a clear plastic container filled with water and large pebbles to raise the water level.

LESSON 11 Fable Origins

Concepts

1. Fables can be found in the oral and written literature of most cultures. The most popular fables in the Western world are supposed to have come from Aesop (e-sop), a slave who lived in ancient Greece.

2. The ancient Hindus and Buddhists of India are probably the world's first and greatest originators of fables. The Book of Five (Panchatantra) was originally written by Hindus to teach religious virtues, but later developed into fables that taught young princes about human nature. The Hitopadesa is a popular version of the Panchatantra. The Jatakas are ancient Buddhist fables from India.

Teaching Strategies

There are many different versions of Aesop's life story. Most fable books and encyclopedias contain a brief account of his life. While nothing is known for certain, it is interesting to compare versions. A good research technique for students is to have each of them read one selection on the life of Aesop from a variety of reference and folklore books. Each could jot down a few interesting details about Aesop's life, along with the title of the resource. Then conduct a sharing time. Start with the information about his early life, recording the facts in a narrative style on a blackboard or overhead; call attention to inconsistencies. Children should stand and tell (not read) their fact. This exercise will not only help students examine the origin of Aesop's fables; it will also help them model the technique for writing a research paper.

Throughout history many writers have used the fable format to express their ideas. Leonardo da Vinci, surprisingly, wrote many fables. Another teller of fables was Jean de La Fontaine (1621-1695), a talented French writer. De La Fontaine, who used Aesop's fables and the Indian Fables of Bidpai as a basis for his very popular fable collection, added poetic verse to the fables. (There are some conflicting accounts of his life that might interest older students who could do independent research.)

Many cultures have fable-type stories in their repertoire of folklore. Since most short folktales contain an object lesson, it can be difficult to decide what is a fable and what is just a folktale.

The fables of India are extensive, quite ancient, and as much a part of the Indian literary tradition as Aesop's work is in the West. Interestingly, some scholars think that the fables attributed to Aesop may have originated in India.

Read aloud these Indian fables:
"The Donkey in the Lion's Skin," page 55
"The Hare and the Rumor," page 56
"The Golden Goose," page 57

From *Fabulous Fables: Using Fables with Children*, published by Good Year Books. Copyright © 1991 Linda K. Garrity.

"The Elephant and the Carpenters," page 58

Ask the class: Would any of these fables support the theory that some of Aesop's fables may have originated in India? Which fables? In what ways are these stories similar to Aesop's? On the other hand, since basic good behavior and common sense are about the same everywhere, is it more reasonable to assume that stories with similar parts could have originated in more than one place?

Now have children brainstorm general similarities and differences between Eastern and Western fables. (One primary difference is the finality of the ending in Aesop's stories–in many Indian fables the characters profit from their lessons and continue on to learn other lessons, though this will not be apparent from the particular fables in this book.)

Enrichment Activity

Crossword Puzzle: Activity Page 18 is a crossword puzzle, featuring animals from the Indian fables. This puzzle is more difficult than the earlier one.

LESSON 12 Modern Fables

Concept

Today many writers use the fable format to present their stories. Indeed, a number of children's books are considered to be fables. Some writers have used the fable format to write humorous parodies or "take-offs" of fables.

Teaching Strategies

Leo Lionni is one of the more famous writer/illustrators of children's picture books that are also considered fables. If possible, read aloud his book *Frederick* (Pantheon, 1967). Then read "The Ant and the Grasshopper," page 54. Ask the class: How do these two stories compare? Which moral do you think more accurately reflects your feelings? (Eric Carle had a strong feeling about this fable–see his *Twelve Fables from Aesop*.)

Arnold Lobel's award winning book *Fables* is a delight for people of all ages. It is a humorous collection of original fables based on the Aesop model. *Foxy Fables,* Tony Ross' fable book, is more a take-off on specific Aesop's fables. *The Exploding Frog* is an amusing rendition of Aesop, and it is closer to the originals than *Foxy Fables.*

For a fun writing exercise, ask students to write their own fables. These can be humorous original fables with old or new proverbs; or they can be parodies or updates on Aesop's fables, using different characters or different settings but keeping the same proverbs.

Read aloud the four made-up fables at the end of this book's section of fable texts, or make copies for children to read to themselves. Ask the children to choose the better proverb for each fable. These fables can also serve as simple examples of humorous fable parodies.

Fables, like all forms of folk literature, hold a natural appeal for children as well as adults. By specifically "zeroing in" on them in a concentrated study, teachers make fables much more memorable for children. Fables have a special place in our literary heritage; after all, the wit and wisdom of our ancestors is certainly equal to the wit and wisdom of our era.

Culminating Activities (pages 61-78)

Craft: Puppets: Puppet shows to accompany fables are an excellent idea because they will work for all ages of children. Culminating Activity Page 1 shows several samples of interesting puppets to make. Only the first one requires any supplies beyond standard school materials.

Writing: Puppet Plays: Writing puppet plays is a different activity from the creative dramatics used in impromptu shows. Culminating Activity 2 is a written play script for "The Stag and the Hedgehog" that can be used as a model for this writing form.

Craft: Peek Boxes: Children can make scenes of fables using large shoeboxes or other boxes. They can cut a large hole in the top of the box, covering the hole with light-colored tissue paper to make a

From Fabulous Fables: Using Fables with Children, published by Good Year Books. Copyright © 1991 Linda K. Garrity.

skylight. Or, they can cut holes in either the top or the bottom of the box for a flashlight. Flashlights are popular, but the tissue paper technique is simpler. Adult help may be needed to help cut the peek-hole in the end of the box.

Craft: Animal Patterns: Culminating Activity Page 3 contains animal patterns for the majority of the animals mentioned in fables. These can be used in a wide variety of ways: with color, detail, and popsickle sticks, they can become stick puppets for younger children; mounted on heavier paper, they could be a part of shadow puppet shows; enlarge them and cut lined paper in the same shape and they are shape books for children to write in; enlarge them or use the same size, depending on the space, and they can be used as a border for a "Fables" bulletin board; use them in any project where the emphasis is on an aspect of children's creativity other than drawing.

Art: Mobiles: Culminating Activity Page 4 shows a number of techniques for making mobiles.

Art: Murals: Painting or coloring murals to show the various stories studied is fun for kids and also is a good review. There are enough fables that each child or pair of children will have a different story to illustrate. Help the children plan the murals so that each scene flows into the next. Indian fables should be grouped together, as well as forest, river, and field sections. They can add titles, though older children should be able to identify the fables without them. If at all possible, allow a small committee to organize the project; this is "real life" problem-solving.

Game: Who Am I?: A charade-type game can be lots of fun for youngsters and at the same time, an excellent review of the fables. It can be as simple as having each child give a first-person clue, with the class trying to guess the fable, or more complicated, with teams and both title and proverb required to win the round.

Game: The Moral Majority Card Game: See Culminating Activity Page 5 for a card game that can be made and played like any "pairs" type of card game. The cards can also be used in a "memory" type of game as well.

Game: Fable Word Search: See Culminating Activity Page 6 for a word search using twenty of the animals most commonly found in fables. Older children might enjoy creating their own crosswords and word searches.

Writing: A simple book report form for younger children helps them record the essence of a fable they have read in an appealing manner. See Culminating Activity Page 7.

Note: Some activities require students to cut out items from the activity page. To give these items more substance, ask the students to glue these items to light cardboard before cutting.

Name: _____   Activity Page 1

The Tortoise and the Hare

Directions:

Color, cut out, and glue animals on paper cups. Use a nail to make a hole in the bottom center of each cup. Tie one end of strings to back of chair. Object of the game: Slide cups so they race to the chair. First player whose cup touches the back of the chair wins.

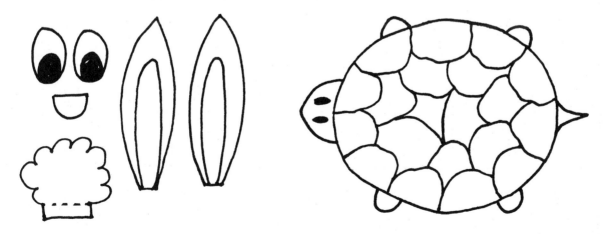

From *Fabulous Fables: Using Fables with Children*, published by Good Year Books. Copyright © 1991 Linda K. Garrity.

Name: _____

Activity Page 2

The Tortoise and the Hare Race

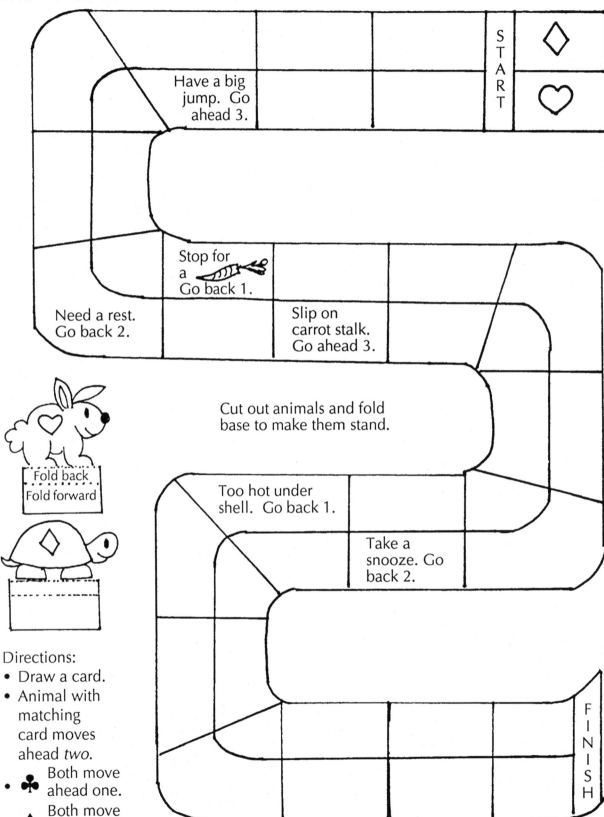

Directions:
- Draw a card.
- Animal with matching card moves ahead *two*.
- ♣ Both move ahead one.
- ♠ Both move back one.

From *Fabulous Fables: Using Fables with Children,* published by Good Year Books. Copyright © 1991 Linda K. Garrity.

Name: _____   **Activity Page 3**

Cross Stitch Sampler on Graph Paper

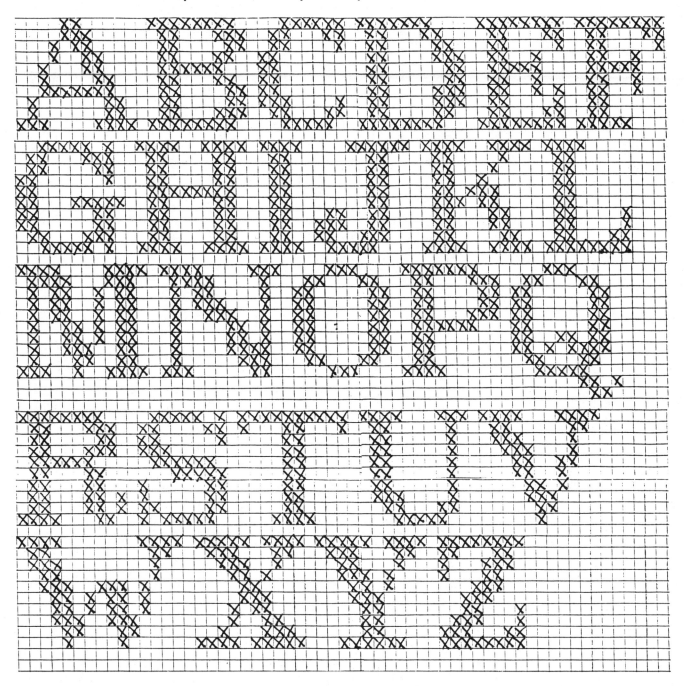

Directions:

Give each child an alphabet pattern and a sheet of graph paper. Using a ruler, draw a one-inch border around the edge. Choose a proverb to illustrate.
Help children plan the approximate centering of the proverb. Fill in the squares with Xs to copy letters. Use pencil. Trace over all penciled Xs with colored pencils or fine-tip markers. Mount on larger piece of construction paper.

From *Fabulous Fables: Using Fables with Children*, published by Good Year Books. Copyright © 1991 Linda K. Garrity.

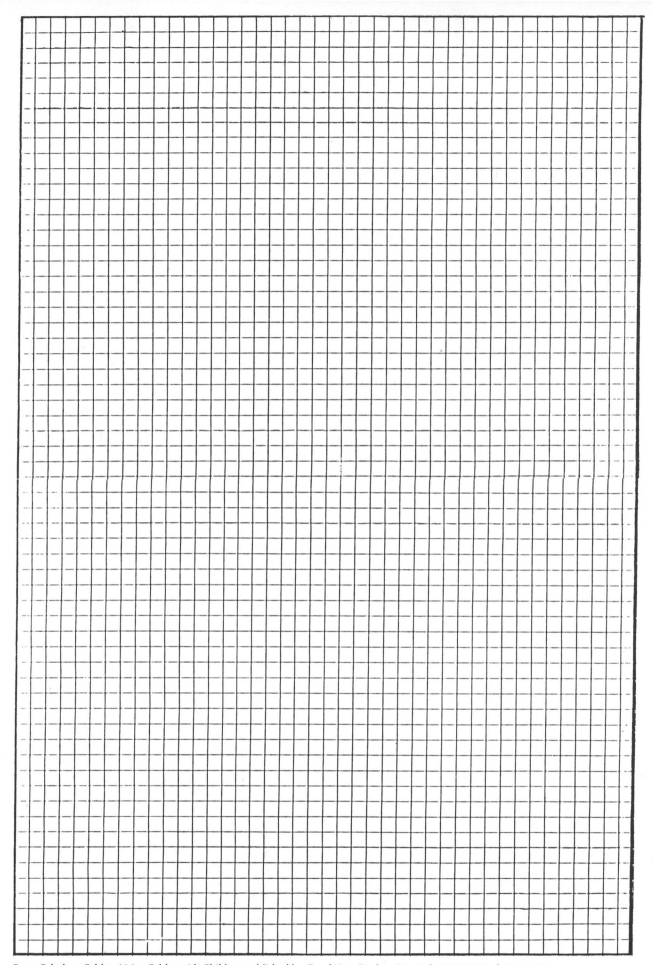

From *Fabulous Fables: Using Fables with Children*, published by Good Year Books. Copyright © 1991 Linda K. Garrity.

Activity Page 4

Name:_____

The Crow and the Pitcher

Directions:

Cut out the pebbles, which describe the crow. Glue them inside the pitcher in ABC order from top to bottom. They may overlap.

- inventive
- thirsty
- smart
- creative
- persistent
- clever
- patient
- hard-working

From *Fabulous Fables: Using Fables with Children,* published by Good Year Books. Copyright © 1991 Linda K. Garrity.

The Lion & the Mouse

Directions:

Help Mouse free Lion by chewing his way through the rope maze.

Name: _____

Activity Page 6

The Ant & the Dove

A very thirsty ant scrambled to the edge of the brook for a fresh drink of water. Then . . .

1.	Dove snips a leaf and swoops down.
2.	Ant sees a hunter aim at Dove.
3.	Ant slips into the current. Help!
4.	Ant bites the hunter and saves Dove. Ouch!
5.	Ant crawls on the leaf and floats to shore.

Directions:

Cut out the pictures. Glue them into the correct sequence on the left.

From *Fabulous Fables: Using Fables with Children*, published by Good Year Books. Copyright © 1991 Linda K. Garrity.

Name: _____   Activity Page 7

Androcles & The Lion

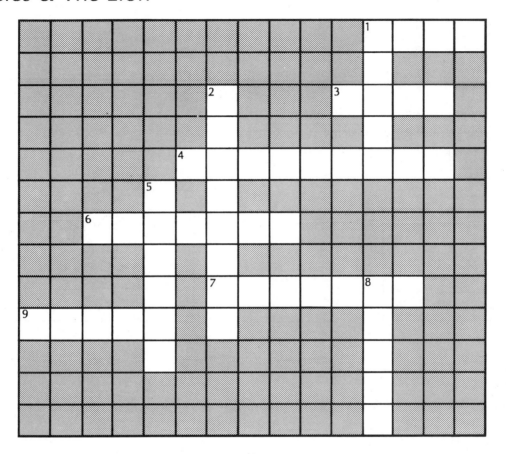

Across Clues

1. The lion brought back fresh _ _ _ _ to Androcles.
3. The "thumbs up" signal meant that Androcles could go _ _ _ _.
4. At first _ _ _ _ _ _ _ _ _ was afraid of the lion.
6. Androcles and the lion were good _ _ _ _ _ _ _.
7. The emperor thought Androcles possessed magic _ _ _ _ _ _ _.
9. A _ _ _ _ _ is a person who is owned by another person.

Down Clues

1. A _ _ _ _ _ is what we call the lesson learned in a fable.
2. No act of _ _ _ _ _ _ _ _ ever goes unrewarded.
5. The lion ran to the center and _ _ _ _ _ _ Androcles' hand.
8. The poor lion had a _ _ _ _ _ imbedded in his paw.

Answers:

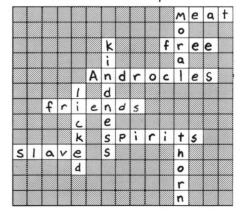

From *Fabulous Fables: Using Fables with Children*, published by Good Year Books. Copyright © 1991 Linda K. Garrity.

Name: _____   Activity Page 8

Sunshine Windsock

Combine the Wind and the Sun with this project.

You need:
  1 12" x 18" piece of yellow construction paper
  1 12" x 18" piece of orange construction paper
  1 2" x 18" tagboard strip
  yellow tissue paper strips
  scissors, glue, and string

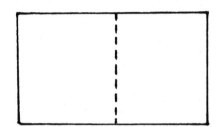  

Directions:

Fold orange construction paper in half as shown. Draw half of sunshine on fold and cut out.

Glue orange paper onto yellow construction paper. Using orange scraps, cut out and glue on sunshine face.

Glue tagboard strip across top of back of yellow paper. Roll two sheets into tube. Glue or staple to hold.

Glue yellow tissue paper strips around bottom of tube. Attach string on either side to hang.

From *Fabulous Fables: Using Fables with Children*, published by Good Year Books. Copyright © 1991 Linda K. Garrity.

Name: _____ Activity Page 9

The Dog and His Shadow Bulletin Board

This fable has many descriptive words. Make a bulletin board of bones with one adjective on each bone.

Use this pattern. Have each child write one adjective from the story on each bone.

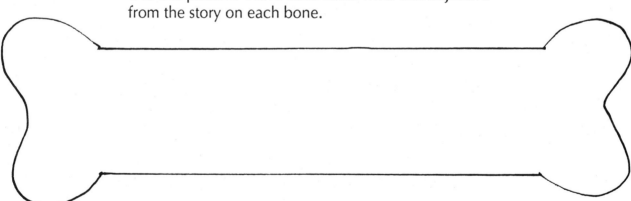

Possible words: large, meaty, safe, quiet, juicy, narrow, slow, clear, quiet, huge, fine.

Option: Write an adjective that describes dogs, such as faithful, friendly, alert, active, playful, etc.

From *Fabulous Fables: Using Fables with Children,* published by Good Year Books. Copyright © 1991 Linda K. Garrity.

Name: _____   Activity Page 10

The Town Mouse and the Country Mouse
Directions:
Draw and color the background for each mouse.

Country Mouse

Town Mouse

From *Fabulous Fables: Using Fables with Children*, published by Good Year Books. Copyright © 1991 Linda K. Garrity.

Name: _____

Activity Page 11

The Farmer and the Hare

Directions:

Write the farmer's dreams in the correct sequence.

- Spend the day drinking tea
- Sell the hare at the market
- Large pig has 12 piglets
- Catch the hare
- Have many sons
- Buy a large pig
- Build a big house
- Piglets have 12 piglets

What happened at the end of the story?

_____
_____
_____
_____
_____

From *Fabulous Fables: Using Fables with Children*, published by Good Year Books. Copyright © 1991 Linda K. Garrity.

The Goose that Laid the Golden Egg

Directions:

Fill the egg with words and pictures of things that are important to you. Color the egg gold or yellow.

From *Fabulous Fables: Using Fables with Children*, published by Good Year Books. Copyright © 1991 Linda K. Garrity.

Name: _____

Activity Page 13

The Fox and the Stork

Directions:

Color the characters. Cut them out. Think carefully about where they belong. Bend the tabs back and glue them on the next page.

From *Fabulous Fables: Using Fables with Children*, published by Good Year Books. Copyright © 1991 Linda K. Garrity.

Activity Page 13 (continued)

Scene 2

Moral _____
_____
_____

Scene 1

From *Fabulous Fables: Using Fables with Children,* published by Good Year Books. Copyright © 1991 Linda K. Garrity.

Name: _____   **Activity Page 14**

The Monkey and the Crocodile
Directions: Cut on solid lines. Fold on dotted lines.

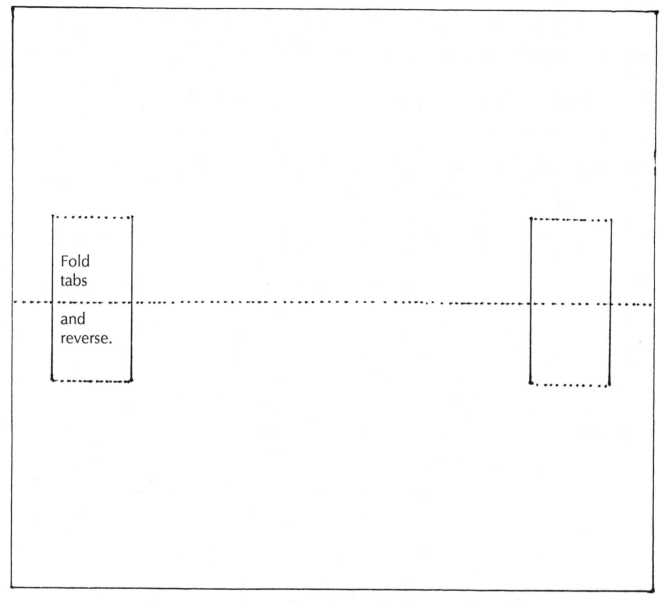

Tie string from one tree to the other. Attach monkey to string.

Fold and glue to base.

Glue trees to front of folded tabs.

From *Fabulous Fables: Using Fables with Children,* published by Good Year Books. Copyright © 1991 Linda K. Garrity.

Name: _____   Activity Page 15

The Fox and the Sick Lion

Directions:

1. Cut out the two 4-1/2" x 6-1/2" cards along the heavy black lines. Fold each in half. Cut across heavy black line of lion's mouth. Fold back the flaps to form two triangles.

Inside card

Outside card

2. Open the flaps and push out to form mouth inside the card. When you open and close the card the mouth will open and close. Glue the inside and outside cards together so you can see the animals when the mouth is open.

From *Fabulous Fables: Using Fables with Children*, published by Good Year Books. Copyright © 1991 Linda K. Garrity.

Name: _____   **Activity Page 16**

ABLE FABLE COMPANY
Employment Application

Name: Big Bad Wolf
Position: Chicken Nuggers,
Previous Work Experiences: Ate Grandmother and Little Red Riding Hood, 7even kids too.
Special Skills & Talents: very Convincing in sheep's clothing.
Health History: Enlarged eyes and teeth, large stones in stomach.
Education: School of Hard Knocks, University of H.O.W.L.
Telephone: 223-9053 BAD

ABLE FABLE COMPANY
Employment Application

Name: _____
Position: _____
Previous Work Experiences: _____
_____
_____
Special Skills & Talents: _____
_____
_____
Health History: _____
_____
Education: _____
_____
Telephone: ___-____

ABLE FABLE COMPANY
Employment Application

Name: _____
Position: _____
Previous Work Experiences: _____
_____
_____
Special Skills & Talents: _____
_____
_____
Health History: _____
_____
Education: _____
_____
Telephone: ___-____

ABLE FABLE COMPANY
Employment Application

Name: _____
Position: _____
Previous Work Experiences: _____
_____
_____
Special Skills & Talents: _____
_____
_____
Health History: _____
_____
Education: _____
_____
Telephone: ___-____

From *Fabulous Fables: Using Fables with Children*, published by Good Year Books. Copyright © 1991 Linda K. Garrity.

Name: _____   Activity Page 17

Quotation Marks in Fables

Directions: Quotation marks are used to indicate that someone is speaking. Add quotation marks to the following dialogue from fables.

    I'd never thought of it that way before, replied the Country Mouse. I've always been happy here.
    I know! Why don't you come visit me and taste all the marvelous food and see the excitement that I enjoy every day in the city? suggested the Town Mouse.
    Very well, said the Country Mouse, I'll come to the city tomorrow.

    Why are you guarding this hay so fiercely? questioned the cows. You cannot eat it yourself and we are quite hungry.
    I am hungry also, replied the self-centered dog, and since I can't eat this hay, I'm not going to let you eat any of it either!

    Aha! exclaimed the Sun. I have an idea. Let's have a contest to see which of us can be the first to make that traveller remove his cloak.
    Very well, said the North Wind, which of us should start first?
    I am so certain of my power, replied the Sun, that I will allow you to go first.

    Now, we are ready to disperse the spoil, said the lion. The first share will, of course, go to me as befits the King of Beasts. The second share will naturally be mine because of the leading role I played in the hunt. It is only fair that the third share fall to me because of my strength and effort in the division of the game.
    And now, growled the lion ominously, as he flexed his claws, for the last portion. If any of you animals feels that it should belong to you, please feel free to speak up now.

    Wife, Wife, look what the old goose has laid! exclaimed the peasant as he ran into the tiny cottage.
    We're rich! We're rich! cried his wife. Just think of the fine things we can buy!

From *Fabulous Fables: Using Fables with Children*, published by Good Year Books. Copyright © 1991 Linda K. Garrity.

Name: _____   Activity Page 18

Indian Fable Animals

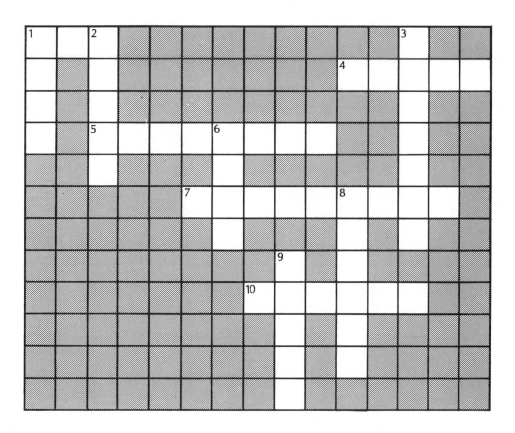

Across Clues

1. ___ in the Hat.
4. Mickey _ _ _ _ _.
5. Memory like an _ _ _ _ _ _ _ _.
7. After while, _ _ _ _ _ _ _ _ _.
10. _ _ _ _ _ _ see, _ _ _ _ _ _ do.

Down Clues

1. Eat _ _ _ _.
2. Catch a _ _ _ _ _ by the tail.
3. _ _ _ _ _ _ _ wings.
6. Tortoise and the _ _ _ _.
8. Pin the tail on the _ _ _ _ _ _.
9. Mother _ _ _ _ _.

Answers: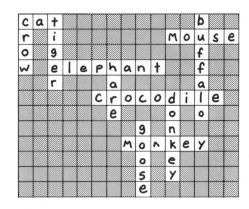

From *Fabulous Fables: Using Fables with Children,* published by Good Year Books. Copyright © 1991 Linda K. Garrity.

Fable Texts

The Tortoise and the Hare

One day a hare was teasing a tortoise in front of the other animals of the forest.

"I am the fastest animal in the forest," boasted he. "No creature could possibly beat me in a race, especially a tortoise like you."

To all the animals' surprise, the slow-moving tortoise retorted, "You are quick, it is true. But I could beat you in a race."

"You? Why, you pokey old thing, hauling your home around on your back, how could you even think of beating a swift hare like myself?" said the hare. "Let's do race and I will prove to you and all the animals of the forest who is the swiftest of all."

The badger was selected to set the course. She picked a route that ran alongside a carrot patch all the way to the big oak tree and back again.

The two animals lined up at the starting gate, the owl signaled, "Go!", and the race was on.

In no time the hare was far ahead of the tortoise. So far ahead, in fact, that he decided to stop and nibble a few tasty carrots from the garden patch. After filling his stomach with the delicious snack, the rabbit laid down in the shade and drifted off to sleep for a long afternoon nap.

Suddenly he awoke, hearing the forest animals shouting. Looking down the race course, he could see that pokey old tortoise slowly plodding toward the finish line. Quickly, the hare jumped up and zoomed toward the finish line, only to see the tortoise win by a length.

MORAL: Slow and steady wins the race.

The Stag and the Hedgehog

A stag and a hedgehog owned a wheat field together. All spring and summer they farmed without a problem. As the wheat began to ripen, they noticed that other animals were getting into the field and eating the golden grains of ripening wheat.

The stag and the hedgehog were both quite upset.

"At this rate," cried the hedgehog angrily, "there will not be a grain left by harvest time."

"Those thieving animals have no respect for another's hard work," the stag replied.

The pair quickly agreed that the stag, being the bigger animal, should stand guard over the field until it was time for harvest.

At first all seemed to go well. Then the hedgehog noticed that the grain was

From *Fabulous Fables: Using Fables with Children,* published by Good Year Books. Copyright © 1991 Linda K. Garrity.

once again being trampled and eaten. He quietly watched the field one evening and saw several deer approach the wheat field. They called greetings to the stag and he came right over, acknowledging his old friends from the meadow. Soon they were all talking, laughing, and eating the wheat together like old times.

The hedgehog was furious. The next day he approached the stag.

"A fine guard you make!" he shouted angrily. "Tomorrow evening I shall take over guarding the field so we can eat next winter."

And the little hedgehog, by the very force of his personality, snarled and growled and bristled until the other larger animals left the wheat field alone.

Soon it was time for the harvest. Once again the stag and the hedgehog cooperated with one another until the wheat was stacked in a large pile.

"Of course, I will need a much larger portion of grain since I am a much larger animal," said the stag.

"Left up to your guarding of the field," returned the hedgehog, "we would not have any wheat to divide. Besides, I may be small, but I have a large family to feed."

The animals continued to argue until a goat wondered by. The stag immediately called him over to render a third opinion. The goat agreed to mediate the dispute, providing both animals would abide by his decision.

"Since you have such difficulty making a decision together," said the crafty goat, "you should run a race with the winner taking all."

"This is an outrage!" thundered the incensed hedgehog. "A tiny animal like me racing a swift stag like him!"

After the hedgehog huffed away for home, the goat turned to the stag and negotiated a sizable percentage of grain for himself.

"We're ruined," cried the hedgehog to his wife, after he had explained the whole story.

"Not so fast," returned his clever wife. "I have a little plan for those two." And she began to explain her scheme to her husband.

That afternoon the two animals started their race. The stag, ever confident that his long legs would ensure his victory, loped swiftly along the course.

Suddenly, he looked up ahead to the finish line, only to see the little hedgehog scurry over the line before him. He was completely baffled, but had to admit defeat.

Later, as the hedgehog couple generously passed out grain to their friends and relatives, the hedgehog wife chuckled, "Those two crooks think all us hedgehogs look alike. I didn't think the stag would notice if I slipped in ahead of him and ran the last leg of the race!"

MORAL: *You may need to cheat to deal with cheaters.*

From *Fabulous Fables: Using Fables with Children,* published by Good Year Books. Copyright © 1991 Linda K. Garrity.

The Crow and the Pitcher

There had been a long dry spell and all the animals were thirsty, especially the crow. Suddenly she saw a pitcher of water sitting on the windowsill of a cottage in the woods. The crow flew over immediately and looked down into the pitcher.

"Ah, there's fresh, cool water in there," she cawed delightedly.

The crow tried to dip her bill down into the pitcher to drink, but could not reach the water because the pitcher only had a small amount in the bottom.

"I'll push the pitcher over," thought the crow, "and then even if some of the water spills to the ground, I'll still get enough for a drink."

Sadly, the earthenware pitcher was too heavy to even budge.

"I have an idea, but it will take a while," thought the crow to herself after more consideration.

She flew away to find pebbles, which she scooped up into her beak, and then flew back to the pitcher to drop the pebbles in. As the pitcher slowly filled with pebbles, the water level began to rise to the brim.

Finally the water level was high enough to allow the crow to quench her thirst.

"This involved much labor," she thought to herself as she thirstily drank the water, "but was well worth it."

MORAL: Necessity is the mother of invention. or Where there's a will, there's a way.

The Lion and the Mouse

The mighty lion was dozing in the sun one afternoon when a small mouse accidently scurried over his nose in her quest for food.

"What's this creature?" roared the lion as his huge paw clamped down over the frightened mouse.

"It is only I, a tiny mouse. Please don't kill me!" begged the mouse. "Besides, it would be beneath the dignity of a mighty king such as yourself to kill an undersized beast like me."

"You have a point there. I do have an image to maintain," agreed the lion as he released the mouse.

"Thank you, O mighty king," replied the diminutive rodent as she dusted herself off before taking her leave. "You won't regret this act of kindness. I will repay you someday."

"Oh, certainly," mocked the lion derisively, as he thought of such a small creature aiding the all-powerful king of the jungle.

Several days later while hunting prey, the lion was ensnared in the ropes of

From *Fabulous Fables: Using Fables with Children,* published by Good Year Books. Copyright © 1991 Linda K. Garrity.

a hunter's trap. The more he struggled to free himself, the worse he became entangled in the ropes. The lion's roars of frustration and anger filled the jungle. The mouse recognized the roars and rushed to the king's aid.

"If you will kindly calm down and lie still, I can accomplish this task more efficiently," said the mouse to the lion as she quickly sized up the situation and started gnawing on the correct ropes.

Soon the last rope was cut and the lion was set free.

"Thank you little one. You were so right when you said that you would repay me someday," said the lion humbly.

MORAL: *Little friends can be great friends.   or   The small can be mighty.*

The Ant and the Dove

A very thirsty ant scrambled to the edge of a brook for a fresh drink of water. In his haste he stumbled, slipped into the current, and was swiftly carried downstream.

"Help! Help! Save me, I'm drowning!" cried the poor ant piteously.

A lovely grey dove was flying above the brook when she heard the desperate cries of the ant. Thinking quickly, the dove snipped off a broad, flat leaf with her bill and swooped down to the water, dropping the leaf beside the ant. The ant crawled up on the leaf and floated to shore like a shipwrecked sailor.

While out searching for food several days later, the ant noticed a hunter taking aim with his gun. Looking skyward, the ant realized that the hunter's prey was none other than the grey dove who had earlier saved his life. Thinking quickly, the ant crawled up the man's shoe and sock and bit him ferociously on his leg.

"Ouch!" shouted the man as he lowered his gun and rubbed his leg.

Meanwhile the lovely dove flew over the treetops to safety.

MORAL: *One good turn deserves another.*

Androcles and the Lion

Once long ago a Greek slave named Androcles ran away after being treated very cruelly by his master. Wandering through the forest, he happened upon a large lion. At first he was terribly frightened and started to run away. When Androcles realized that the lion had made no attempt to pursue him and, in fact, seemed barely able to raise his head, the

From *Fabulous Fables: Using Fables with Children,* published by Good Year Books. Copyright © 1991 Linda K. Garrity.

slave crept back to investigate. He soon saw that the problem was a badly infected paw.

Summoning up all his courage, Androcles kindly offered, "May I be of some service to you, O king of beasts?"

The lion extended his throbbing paw for treatment.

"I think you have a sharp thorn embedded between these two toes. I will remove the thorn as gently as possible," explained the slave sympathetically.

The removal of the thorn brought such relief that the lion licked Androcles' hand in gratitude. Androcles then bandaged the paw with strips of his own garment and decided to stay with the lion to tend the injury. The lion soon recovered and brought back fresh meat each day from his hunts for both of them.

One day while the lion was out hunting, the poor slave was captured and taken to the city for the circus. Unbeknownst to Androcles the lion was also captured that day and was kept without food in a small cage so that he would ferociously attack the victims in the arena.

On the day of the circus the stands were filled with spectators. The unlucky slave was selected as the first victim and was hauled to the center of the arena. At the Emperor's signal the first lion was released and raced toward the hapless victim. To everyone's astonishment the huge lion, instead of tearing the slave limb from limb, began to lick the hand of his old friend. The crowd roared their surprise and approval, so the Emperor summoned Androcles to him.

"What magic spirits do you possess to tame wild beasts?" he asked.

"I have none, sir," Androcles replied modestly. "I saved this lion's life when he was injured."

To the crowd's approval the Emperor gave the "thumbs up" signal, freeing the lion to return to the forest and freeing Androcles from both death and slavery.

MORAL: *No act of kindness, no matter how small, ever goes unrewarded.*
     or   *The small can be mighty.*

The Wind and the Sun

ne day the North Wind and the Sun were arguing about which of them was the stronger of the two. There seemed to be no way of settling this issue. Then both looked down to earth and noticed a traveller walking down the road.

"Aha!" exclaimed the Sun. "I have an idea. Let's have a contest to see which of us can be the first to make that traveller remove his cloak."

"Very well," said the North Wind, "which of us should start first?"

From *Fabulous Fables: Using Fables with Children,* published by Good Year Books. Copyright © 1991 Linda K. Garrity.

"I am so certain of my power," replied the Sun, "that I will allow you to go first."

At that the Sun withdrew behind a cloud and the North Wind started blowing strong icy blasts of wind and, for good measure, mixed in icy driving rain. Instead of having the desired results, this strategy caused the traveller to draw his cloak even more tightly around himself. Finally, the North Wind had to concede defeat.

The Sun started her turn slowly, coming out from behind a cloud and driving the mists from the sky. Once the sky was clear, she was free to spread her rays and beam down over the land.

This proved too warm for the traveller, who finally had to remove his cloak and sit down in the shade before continuing on.

MORAL: *Persuasion is better than force.*

The Lion's Share

The lion usually went hunting alone. He decided one day, however, to invite along a fox, a wolf, and a wild donkey to help in the hunt by running down the prey so that all he had to do was the final kill. This technique worked very well and before long the four animals sat down to divide a nice fat stag that they had bagged.

"Careful, careful," admonished the lion as the animals rushed up to the kill to seize their portions. "Let's divide this meat up equally and distribute it in an organized fashion."

So the other three animals sat back as the lion carefully divided the carcass into four equal portions.

"Now, we are ready to disperse the spoil," said the lion. "The first share will, of course, go to me as befits the King of the Beasts. The second share will naturally be mine because of the leading role I played in the hunt. It is only fair that the third share fall to me because of my strength and effort in the division of the game."

"And now," growled the lion ominously, as he flexed his claws, "for the last portion. If any of you animals feels that it should belong to you, please feel free to speak up now."

MORAL: *Might makes right.*

From *Fabulous Fables: Using Fables with Children*, published by Good Year Books. Copyright © 1991 Linda K. Garrity.

The Dog and His Shadow

The dog had stolen a large meaty bone from a butcher shop and was scurrying away to find a safe, quiet place in which to enjoy the juicy morsel. As he crossed a narrow footbridge over a slow, clear stream, he happened to look down at the quiet water at his own reflection.

"Egad!" he thought to himself. "Look at that huge meat bone that dog is carrying in his mouth. Why, if I could get his bone, along with the one I already have, I could really have a fine feast."

With that the dog snarled, barked, and lunged for what he thought was the other dog's bone, dropping his own bone and falling into the stream.

MORAL: Be content with what you have.   or   A bird in the hand is better than two in the bush.

The Goose that Laid the Golden Egg

Once a poor peasant went to check the nest of his only goose to see if there might be an egg for the family's supper. Instead of the usual white egg, a solid gold one lay in its place.

"Wife, wife, look what the old goose has laid!" exclaimed the peasant as he ran into the tiny cottage.

"We're rich! We're rich!" cried his wife. "Just think of the fine things we can buy!"

Each day as they checked the nest, they found a new golden egg. The speculation about what they would purchase with the gold grew more grandiose each day. Finally, their greed reached the point where they were no longer content to build their wealth by one golden egg each day.

"Husband, why must we acquire our wealth this slow, laborious way? Why don't you cut open the old goose so that we may have all the gold at once?" suggested the wife.

At first the husband hemmed and hawed, but finally agreed to butcher the goose and take control of the fortune.

After killing the old goose, the husband brought it into the hut to cut the goose open while his wife watched. Slowly and carefully he worked, only to find–nothing at all.

MORAL: Be content with what you have.   or   The greedy who want more lose all.

From *Fabulous Fables: Using Fables with Children,* published by Good Year Books. Copyright © 1991 Linda K. Garrity.

The Town Mouse and the Country Mouse

Once the elegant Town Mouse came for a visit with her cousin the Country Mouse. The Country Mouse showed her cousin all the local sights, such as the meadow, streams, and the barn. Then she worked all afternoon to prepare her finest meal: acorns, ground roots, and seeds, with cold water for a beverage.

The Town Mouse politely pushed her food around on her plate before she finally said to her cousin, "How can you stand to work so hard for such simple, tasteless fare? And the life-style here in the country–how can you tolerate the boredom?"

"I'd never thought of it that way before," replied the Country Mouse. "I've always been happy here."

"I know! Why don't you come visit me and taste all the marvelous food and see the excitement that I enjoy every day in the city?" suggested the Town Mouse.

"Very well," said the Country Mouse, "I'll come to the city tomorrow."

The next day when they reached the home of the Town Mouse, the two cousins were tired and hungry.

"Let's enjoy a fine meal before we retire for the evening," suggested the Town Mouse. "Follow me into the dining room."

And there on an elegant dining room table lay the remnants of an exquisite feast–ripe fruit, cheeses, fancy breads and crackers, rich desserts, and fine wine to drink. The humble Country Mouse was nearly overcome with astonishment at the richness of her cousin's life-style. However, just as she was about to bite into a sweet grape, a pair of dogs came rushing into the dining room.

"Quick, hide in the sugar bowl!" shouted the Town Mouse.

Finally the dogs gave up and left the room and the mice came out of hiding to try to eat once again. Soon, a huge cat raced into the room and leaped upon the table. They escaped from the cat, only to have the servant girl come into the room to remove the dishes. That was the final straw for the Country Mouse.

Bundling her homespun coat about her as she headed for the doorway, she called to her elegant cousin, "I'm going back to the country as fast as I can. Better a simple life in peace than a luxurious life in fear!"

MORAL: *Be content with what you have.*   or   *A bird in the hand is better than two in the bush.*

From *Fabulous Fables: Using Fables with Children*, published by Good Year Books. Copyright © 1991 Linda K. Garrity.

The Milkmaid and Her Pail

As the young milkmaid made her way to the market with a pail of milk on her head, she began to muse about plans for the money she would receive from the sale of the milk.

The milkmaid thought to herself: "This milk will give me enough money to buy some hens. They will lay eggs, which I will gather and sell. By May I will have sufficient funds to buy myself a lovely new dress to wear to the fair. Green it should be; yes, I will look so lovely in green. All the young men will notice me. They will all want to dance with me. But when they ask me to dance, I will pretend that I am too fine for them. When they insist that I dance, I will toss my head disdainfully." And with that thought, the milkmaid tossed her head.

But alas! As she tossed her head backward, the pail of milk flew off, spilling every drop on the ground. With the milk also disappeared the hens, the eggs, and the green dress.

MORAL: *Don't count your chickens before they hatch.*

The Farmer and the Hare

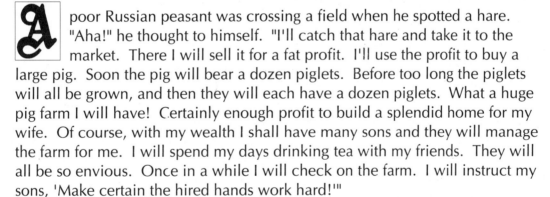A poor Russian peasant was crossing a field when he spotted a hare. "Aha!" he thought to himself. "I'll catch that hare and take it to the market. There I will sell it for a fat profit. I'll use the profit to buy a large pig. Soon the pig will bear a dozen piglets. Before too long the piglets will all be grown, and then they will each have a dozen piglets. What a huge pig farm I will have! Certainly enough profit to build a splendid home for my wife. Of course, with my wealth I shall have many sons and they will manage the farm for me. I will spend my days drinking tea with my friends. They will all be so envious. Once in a while I will check on the farm. I will instruct my sons, 'Make certain the hired hands work hard!'"

"Those lazybones!" shouted the peasant aloud, forgetting himself.

And with that, the hare ran away, taking with him the pig, the piglets, the farm, the house, the sons, and the lazy hired hands.

MORAL: *This Russian story is told as a folktale without a formal moral. What proverb do you think would match?*

From *Fabulous Fables: Using Fables with Children,* published by Good Year Books. Copyright © 1991 Linda K. Garrity.

The Dog in the Manger

A dog was resting in a manger filled with fresh hay. Presently two cows meandered over to the manger to eat their dinner of hay. As they neared the manger, the dog began barking and growling and snapping at them.

"Why are you guarding this hay so fiercely?" questioned the cows. "You cannot eat it yourself and we are quite hungry."

"I am hungry also," replied the self-centered dog, "and since I can't eat this hay, I'm not going to let you eat any of it either!"

MORAL: Live and let live.   or   Don't begrudge others what you yourself cannot enjoy.

The Fox and the Stork

One day a fox invited a stork over to his home for dinner. When the stork arrived, she was promptly shown into the fox's dining room where an exquisite table had been set. After pleasantries were exchanged, the fox seated the stork and went into the kitchen to bring in the main course. And what a fine meal it was, steaming and fragrant, served in two shallow dishes.

The fox expressed her appreciation, "Why, thank you fox, this is one of my favorite recipes."

But, try though she might, she was not able to maneuver her bill for a single bite of the tempting meal.

The sly fox, enjoying his dinner, said, "Here, let me help you with your food."

And soon, he had eaten her dinner as well as his own.

The stork realized she had been tricked, but saw no gain in losing her temper. Instead, she chatted pleasantly, thanked the fox for his hospitality, and departed for home.

The following week the stork invited the fox to her home for dinner. The fox arrived promptly, licking his chops in anticipation of a delicious meal.

After seating the fox, the stork brought in two bowls filled with an appetizing fish dinner. The fox could not wait to dive into the food as he was quite hungry. But alas, the two containers were tall, narrow vases and he could not manage a single bite, while the stork hastily ate her dinner.

"Would you care to have me help you with your portion?" inquired the stork demurely.

"You know I can't get my muzzle into this vase!" exploded the fox. "You have deceived me!"

From *Fabulous Fables: Using Fables with Children,* published by Good Year Books. Copyright © 1991 Linda K. Garrity.

"Now hold on just a minute," returned the stork calmly. "You thought it was a clever trick when you did this to me, but it's not so amusing when the trick is played on you. Next time, don't play tricks on your friends if you can't take it when they play tricks on you."

MORAL: *Don't play tricks on others if you can't stand the same treatment yourself.*

The Fox and the Sick Lion

The lion sent word throughout the forest that he was on his deathbed and wanted all the beasts to stop by his den to pay their last respects.
The fox was busy hunting for food in the forest and did not want to bother with the lion.

Later the hawk flew by to ask the fox why he had not paid his respects to the dying king of the beasts.

"I have stopped by the entrance to the lion's den to pay homage to him several times," explained the fox, "and I always saw the tracks of many different creatures going into the den. I would be very willing to join the other animals in paying last respects to the lion, when I see the same number of tracks leading out again."

MORAL: *Don't believe everything you hear.*   or   *Take warning from the misfortunes of others.*

The Lion, the Wolf, and the Fox

The lion sent word throughout all the forest that he was on his deathbed and wanted all the beasts to stop by his den to pay their last respects.
The fox was busy hunting for food in the forest and did not want to bother with the lion.

The wolf, who was also sly, noticed the absence of the fox and called this to the attention of the lion.

"Your majesty, we have all come to visit you, except the fox. Apparently, he does not care whether you live or die," said the wolf, thinking that he would settle an old grudge with the fox.

The fox came into the den just as the wolf was saying this to the lion and overheard the wolf's conversation.

From *Fabulous Fables: Using Fables with Children,* published by Good Year Books. Copyright © 1991 Linda K. Garrity.

"Fox, you disloyal beast! Why are you just now stopping by to show your concern?" roared the lion in anger.

"Please, your majesty, allow me to explain!" pleaded the fox sincerely. "The reason I have not been here sooner is that I have been searching the world over for a miraculous cure for you."

"And have you found one?" asked the lion anxiously.

"Indeed I have, your majesty," replied the fox. "You must wrap your body in a warm wolf's pelt."

The lion immediately killed the wolf in order to try the fox's prescription.

MORAL: Unkind actions may come back to you.   or   What goes around, comes around.

The Bundle of Sticks

A man had several sons who quarreled endlessly. He tried his best to counsel them against this distressful behavior, all to no avail. He thought and thought about an example that would show his sons the folly of their ways.

Finally, after an especially vicious quarrel among the sons, a plan came to the father. He obtained a large bundle of sticks used for firewood and had them tightly bound together. Then he summoned his sons.

"These are thin, brittle twigs," said the man to his sons. "Please take this bundle and break it in half."

Each son in turn took the bundle of sticks and try though he might, could not even begin to break the bundle in half.

Then the man cut the cord that bound the twigs and gave each son a stick to break. The sticks, of course, snapped in half easily between their fingers.

The father looked at his sons gravely, "Do you not see, my sons, that you are like these sticks? When you all stand together, no enemy can harm you. But when you quarrel and stand divided, then you are easy prey for your enemies."

MORAL: In unity there is strength.   or   United we stand, divided we fall.

From *Fabulous Fables: Using Fables with Children,* published by Good Year Books. Copyright © 1991 Linda K. Garrity.

The Two Travellers and a Bear

Two men who were the best of friends set forth on a journey. They promised that they would help one another to the death in the face of danger.

They had not traveled far along their journey when, suddenly, out of the bushes a huge bear rushed them. The one man, being an able climber, quickly scrambled up into the branches of the nearest tree. His companion, having no chance alone against the bear, dropped to the ground, pretending to be dead. He had remembered hearing that bears will not disturb a dead body.

As he lay there on the forest floor holding his breath and praying, the bear came over to him, sniffed him all around with his muzzle, and finally ambled off into the forest.

After a bit the friend in the tree climbed down and shamefacedly came over to check on his companion.

"That was a close one, wasn't it?" he commented. "I saw the bear put his muzzle close to your ear. Did he whisper something to you?"

"Why, yes he did," replied his friend as he was getting to his feet. "He said that I should not trust friends who make promises in safety but desert their companions in danger."

MORAL: *Misfortune is the true test of friendship.*

The Fox and the Grapes

A hungry fox once came to a vineyard where grapes, heavy and ripe, were hanging from a trellis. Eyeing the luscious grapes from the ground, the fox jumped again and again to reach the fruit. Alas, the fox grew quite weary from his efforts, but could not come even close to the tempting fruit.

At last he turned away in defeat, "Who would want those grapes? They are green, sour things not fit for human or beast!"

MORAL: *It is easy to despise the things one cannot have.*

From *Fabulous Fables: Using Fables with Children,* published by Good Year Books. Copyright © 1991 Linda K. Garrity.

A Wolf in Sheep's Clothing

A wolf decided to disguise himself in a sheep's pelt so that he could hide amongst the flock and eat his fill of sheep.

The trick seemed to work quite well. Covered with the pelt, the wolf stood in the field all day long, pretending to eat grass with the sheep. That night the shepherd unknowingly herded the wolf right into the pen along with the rest of the flock.

Just as the wolf had selected his first sheep to eat, he heard footsteps coming. The shepherd had also decided to kill a sheep for supper that night and quickly slaughtered the largest one in the flock.

The shepherd was quite shocked when he started to skin the sheep, only to find a large, dead wolf.

MORAL: Don't pretend to be what you are not.

The Monkey and the Crocodile

(a much abbreviated version of a Jataka tale from India)

Once near the Himalaya Mountains on the Ganges River there lived a clever monkey who swung from branch to branch, eating fruit all day long.

Swimming in the river and sunning on the bank were many crocodiles. After watching the monkey happily swing along, a crocodile decided that he would like to catch him and eat him.

"How can you do that?" laughed the other crocodiles. "You can't climb trees, and monkeys do not go into the water. Besides monkeys are much quicker than us crocodiles."

"The monkey is quick, you are right," answered the crocodile. "but I am very cunning. We shall see who will be the victor."

So one day when the monkey came to the edge of the Ganges to get a drink, the crocodile, who had been watching him, quickly swam over and inquired, "Monkey, aren't you tired of eating the same old fruit day after day? Wouldn't you like to taste the sweet mangoes in the trees on the other side of the river?"

"Why, yes, I would like to eat that fruit, but I can't reach the other side of the Ganges. I cannot swim," replied the monkey.

"As a special favor to you, I could carry you across on my back," said the crocodile with a toothy grin.

So the monkey hopped onto the broad back of the crocodile and they glided across the wide Ganges River. Soon they came to the middle of the river where it was the deepest and the crocodile started to dive.

From *Fabulous Fables: Using Fables with Children,* published by Good Year Books. Copyright © 1991 Linda K. Garrity.

"Stop! Stop!" screeched the monkey as the crocodile resurfaced. "What are you doing? You know I can't swim a stroke!"

"I'm going to drown you so that I can eat you," replied the crocodile calmly. "You surely don't think I'm doing all this out of the kindness of my heart."

"I'm certainly glad that you told me this now or otherwise you would have been so disappointed," said the monkey.

"Disappointed? How is that?" asked the crocodile.

"The tastiest part of a monkey is the heart and I've left mine behind. We monkeys leap about the trees so much that if we carried our hearts with us, they would become damaged. So we keep them in special places on the trees."

"Well then," said the crocodile. "let's go back to the shore and get your heart. If you give it to me, I'll just eat it and not bother to drown you."

"Very well, I'll get my tasty heart for you as soon as we reach the shore," said the monkey solemnly.

As soon as they reached the shore, the monkey scampered down off the crocodile's back and up the nearest tree.

"Oh, crocodile, I'm up here with my heart!" laughed the monkey. "If you want it, come on up and get it!"

The Boy Who Cried Wolf

very day a shepherd boy was sent to the meadow near the village to tend his flock. The days were long and monotonous and the boy grew very bored. Toward the end of one long, lonely day, he thought of a way to create some excitement.

"Wolf! Wolf!" screamed the boy as he ran toward the village.

"We're coming! We"re coming!" shouted the villagers as they raced toward the meadow with sticks and clubs in their hands to kill the wolf.

The boy laughed gleefully to see the men running with such intensity. When they discovered that there was no wolf and the boy had shouted the alarm only for his amusement, they were very angry.

A short time later the boy again grew bored with his job and sounded the alarm "Wolf! Wolf!"

Again the men came running and again they were disgusted at being tricked.

Finally there came a day when a wolf really did come to raid the flock. The boy screamed and screamed for help.

"Pay no mind to that scoundrel. He's up to his old tricks again," said the villagers as they ignored the boy and went on about their work.

And so the wolf was able to eat the entire flock of sheep at his leisure.

MORAL: *A liar will not be believed, even when he tells the truth.*

From *Fabulous Fables: Using Fables with Children,* published by Good Year Books. Copyright © 1991 Linda K. Garrity.

The Ant and the Grasshopper

ne lovely summer day a grasshopper was dancing and singing, enjoying the beauty of the world around her. Meanwhile an ant scurried by with a large kernel of corn in her jaw.

"Why are you working so hard on such a gorgeous day?" asked the grasshopper. "Why don't you take the day off and enjoy the fresh air and blooming flowers?"

"What are you thinking about? There is a long winter coming up and my relatives and I are storing up all the food we can while it is still plentiful," said the ant disdainfully.

"Oh, I don't even want to think about winter yet, I'm having so much fun enjoying summertime. Besides, many of the insects of the forest really appreciate my musical talents," replied the grasshopper.

The ant shrugged and went on about her way. She and her relatives toiled under the summer sun to set in large stores of food for winter.

Finally winter arrived. Cold winds blew, snow covered the forest and there was nothing to eat.

"Ants! Ants!" called the grasshopper to her friends who were snug in their den, "I am terribly cold and hungry. Won't you share your food with me?"

"We saw you last summer, dancing and singing while we toiled away to lay in stores. We're sorry, but we can't support you. If you insist on playing all summer, then you must starve all winter," answered the ants.

MORAL: *Provide for the future.*   or   *Save for a rainy day.*

The Hermit and the Mouse
(an Indian fable from the Hitopadesa)

here was once a hermit whose prayers were always answered. One day as he sat meditating, he saw a crow sweep down to scoop up a defenseless little mouse in its beak. The hermit jumped up and ran to the mouse's rescue, snatching it from the beak of the crow. He then cradled the frightened creature in his hands and took it home to rest and eat grains of rice. The mouse recovered from its near-disaster and grew contented.

Some time later as the hermit was meditating, he saw a large cat prowling about his hut in pursuit of the mouse. Quickly the hermit prayed and the little mouse was turned into a large, sleek cat which scared away the strange cat.

The hermit enjoyed his new pet and took good care of him. Then one day he heard a dog barking and ran to find his cat in a tree with a dog barking ferociously beneath the tree. The hermit prayed, turning his cat into a dog which

From *Fabulous Fables: Using Fables with Children,* published by Good Year Books. Copyright © 1991 Linda K. Garrity.

immediately pounced upon the other dog, scaring it away.

The hermit enjoyed his new pet and took good care of him. Then one day as the dog was walking in the forest, he came upon a tiger who stiffened his back, preparing to pounce. Again the hermit prayed and turned the dog into a magnificent royal tiger. The new tiger chased the other tiger away and began strutting about the forest, admiring himself. The hermit was kind to the tiger, but he reminded him that the tiger had once been a lowly mouse and to not put on airs. The more the tiger thought about this, the more it bothered him.

Finally, he thought to himself, "If only the hermit were not around to remind me of my humble beginnings, then I could enjoy my splendid life as a powerful royal tiger. I must kill him at once."

With that thought, the tiger strode toward the hermit's hut to kill him. The hermit sensed the tiger's presence and his evil intent, and quickly prayed, turning the arrogant tiger back into a defenseless mouse.

The mouse scurried away into the forest, never to be seen again.

The Donkey in the Lion's Skin

(an Indian tale from the Jatakas)

donkey carried the wares of an old trader who traveled from village to village, selling his goods. When they reached the edge of a village, the trader would remove the baskets of wares from the donkey's back, cover him with a lion's skin, and leave him in the villagers' grain fields to eat his fill at others' expense. The trader would then go on into the village to sell his wares, knowing that his donkey was feeding undisturbed.

One day while the trader was busy in a village and his donkey was busy eating the peasants' grain, a watchful guard saw the "lion" in the fields. Afraid of the "lion", but wanting to save the crops, he sounded an alarm to call the villagers to the field. Quickly they came with clubs and noise-makers to scare the "lion" away.

The "lion," seeing and hearing the commotion, grew frightened and brayed loudly.

The villagers stopped in their tracks at such a sound. This was no fearsome beast, but only a lowly donkey, eating their precious grain. Their outrage grew at the thought of such a trick. Angrily they ran up to the hapless donkey, pulled off the lion's skin, and beat the donkey to death.

The trader, seeing what had happened, quickly packed his wares, hung them on his own back, and beat a hasty retreat out of the village.

From *Fabulous Fables: Using Fables with Children*, published by Good Year Books. Copyright © 1991 Linda K. Garrity.

The Hare and the Rumor

(an Indian fable from the Jatakas)

Once a small hare sat under a fruit tree thinking. "Earthquakes are frightening. They cause the earth to shake and tremble and finally, parts of the earth break apart. I wonder what I should do if an earthquake should start?" pondered the little hare to himself.

As the hare was worrying about this, a ripe piece of fruit fell with a heavy thud just behind him.

"Horrors! It has started! The great earthquake that I was fearing has begun!" the hare shouted aloud.

Quickly he started running around in circles and then sprinted away toward the ocean. On the way he passed another hare.

"What's the matter?" called the hare.

"It's a giant earthquake! Run for your life!" called the first hare to his friend.

So the second hare started running toward the ocean also. Other hares heard the alarm and soon thousands were racing for their lives. The news spread and other species, in turn, sounded the alarm and headed toward the ocean to avoid the great earthquake. The deer, boars, elk, buffaloes, oxen, rhinoceroses, tigers, and elephants all thundered across the Indian terrain.

The clouds of dust and din of the animals awakened a lion in his cave. He looked out of his cave in the hillside to see vast herds of animals in flight.

"What is happening? Where are all the animals going?" asked the lion. When his companion told him that the animals were running from a great earthquake that would break apart the earth, he became deeply worried.

"They are headed straight toward the ocean. If they aren't stopped, they'll all be drowned!" he cried.

The lion raced down the slope to the front of the animal herds and roared the loudest, most frightening roar he could muster. This immediately stopped the animals in their tracks.

"What is the problem here?" the lion fiercely demanded.

"The earth is breaking! The earth is breaking!" cried the hysterical animals.

"This doesn't sound very logical. Let's talk to the largest animals first," reasoned the lion calmly. "Elephants, elephants, tell me what is going on."

"The earth is breaking up from an earthquake," answered the elephants.

"Who told you this?" asked the lion.

"The tigers told us," answered the elephants.

"The rhinoceroses told us," answered the tigers.

"The oxen told us," answered the rhinoceroses.

"The buffaloes told us," answered the oxen.

"The elk told us," answered the buffaloes.

"The boars told us," answered the elk.

"The hares told us," answered the boars.

From *Fabulous Fables: Using Fables with Children*, published by Good Year Books. Copyright © 1991 Linda K. Garrity.

"The little hare told us," answered the hares.

"Is this true," asked the lion to the small hare, "that you told the animals that the earth was breaking up?"

"Oh, yes," answered the little hare, "I heard it with my own ears."

"Where?" asked the lion.

"Under the tree where I live," answered the hare assuredly.

"Hop on my back and take me to the place where this happened," said the lion. "The rest of you animals wait here for my verdict."

With that the lion raced away toward the hare's home with the little hare clinging to the lion's back.

"There!" shouted the little hare. "Under that big tree just ahead."

The lion walked cautiously under the tree and searched carefully, but the only thing he could find was a large, very ripe piece of fruit.

"This must have been the cause of all this—a piece of fruit falling to the ground," said the lion as he turned to race back to the waiting animals.

When he returned, he said to the animals, "It was only ripe fruit falling to the ground. The earth is not breaking up, nor is there an earthquake. I ask you animals now, which is worse: the one who starts a rumor or the one who believes it?"

The Golden Goose

(an Indian fable from the Jatakas)

nce there was a poor man with a wife and three daughters. When he died, his widow and daughters were desperately poor and had to rely on the charity of their neighbors to avoid starving.

One morning after an especially long hungry night the family awoke to find a large magnificent goose with feathers of spun gold resting on the hearth.

"What are you?" asked the daughters in awe.

"I am your beloved father," replied the goose, "reborn in this form to save you from poverty and misery. I will give you my golden feathers, one by one, so that you can live in comfort for the rest of your days."

Then he flew swiftly away, dropping a single feather of spun gold for his family. The mother, who was a hard-hearted sort, quickly snatched up the feather and took it to the market to trade for food and clothing, especially fine gowns for herself.

The family lived well for some time until their funds dwindled. Then the golden goose reappeared and left another golden feather, just before the cupboard grew bare. Again and again the family's funds depleted, only to be replenished by yet another feather from the goose.

The greedy mother became impatient with this slow method of support.

From *Fabulous Fables: Using Fables with Children,* published by Good Year Books. Copyright © 1991 Linda K. Garrity.

One day she said to her daughters, "How can we trust this goose to continue to drop feathers for us? What if it is killed or changes its mind? Then we would be reduced to poverty once again. No, I say we should capture the goose the next time it appears, pluck all its golden feathers, and thus assure ourselves of our fortune."

"Oh no, mother," cried the horrified daughters. "The goose is our father, he would never desert us. And to pluck all his feathers would wound him. We could never do that to father."

Unfortunately, the next time the goose came to the cottage to leave a feather, the mother was the only one at home. Quickly, she seized the goose, plucked out every one of his golden feathers, and flung him out onto the trash heap. She gathered the feathers into a large basket and sat down to admire her treasure. But lo and behold, in the basket lay not a vast golden treasure, but only a pile of plain, white goose feathers.

The Elephant and the Carpenters

(an Indian fable from the Jatakas)

nce long ago in India there was a village where all the men were carpenters. These carpenters would travel to the great forests and harvest the timber for a living.

One day an elephant, trying to escape the heat of the day, rested in the shade near where the carpenters were sawing planks out of logs. As the elephant stepped near some scraps of wood, he stepped on a huge splinter. The splinter became infected, causing the elephant great pain.

A few days later the carpenters noticed the elephant limping and then they saw the splinter sticking out of the poor animal's foot.

"Here," they said, "let us remove that splinter for you. Your poor foot needs to be cleaned and bandaged as well, so that you can once again walk."

The carpenters tended the elephant's wound each day until it had healed. The elephant never forgot the kindness of the carpenters. Each day he came to help them with the heavy work of dragging logs and loading the planks ready for sale. Each of the carpenters, in turn, shared some of his food with the elephant to keep him healthy and able.

To this day elephants work hard in India, doing heavy work for men who love them and feed them well.

From *Fabulous Fables: Using Fables with Children,* published by Good Year Books. Copyright © 1991 Linda K. Garrity.

The Report Card

Two girls were hurrying to school. It was the last day of the school year and they were anxious to get their report cards.

"My mom is going to give me 50 cents for every 'A' and 25 cents for every 'B'," said the first girl. "I can hardly wait to get my card. I know I'll get an 'A' in math and spelling and reading and art. And I'm sure I'll get a 'B' in language and music. Let's see, how much will that be?"

The girls stopped and took out pencils and paper to figure up the total.

"$2.50! Wow, with that money I could take both of us skating," said the first girl.

The two girls met after school to walk home together.

"How did you do on your report card?" asked the second girl.

"Just like I said I would," said the first girl. "So let's see if we can go skating tomorrow."

"Okay. I'll bring my allowance and buy us both snacks then," the second girl replied excitedly. "My mom always says..."

...don't count your chickens before they hatch.   or   *...one good turn deserves another.*

The Sneakers

A mother took her two excited sons to the shoe store to buy tennis shoes. There were many styles to choose from, but finally both boys decided upon a special pair of white shoes with red and blue racing stripes.

When the shoe salesman returned from the storage room to fit the boys, he had only one box of shoes in his hands.

"Sorry, son. We don't have this style in your size," he said to the older boy. Then he sat down and tried the shoes on the younger boy. They were a perfect fit.

"Wow! These are neat. I want to get these, Mom," exclaimed the younger boy.

The older boy looked at his brother frisking around in his new shoes and then said, "Those racing stripes are just for girls. All the guys at school will laugh at you in those."

The mother looked at the salesman and commented, "I think we have a case here of..."

...the goose that laid the golden egg.   or   *...sour grapes.*

From *Fabulous Fables: Using Fables with Children,* published by Good Year Books. Copyright © 1991 Linda K. Garrity.

Lunch

everal children were eating their lunch together in the school cafeteria. One girl commented on the apricots that had been served for dessert, "Yuck! I hate apricots. They are so mushy."

"Oh, I just love apricots," said her friend. "May I have yours?"

"No, you can't," replied the first girl as she scraped her apricots into the trash bin.

Another child had been watching the two girls during lunch and when they left the cafeteria, she said, "That girl is a real..."

...dog in the manger.   or   ...wolf in sheep's clothing.

The Boy and His Mother

One morning the boy called to his mother from his bed, "Mother, I'm sick! My stomach hurts and I think I have a fever. I can't go to school."

His mother debated what to do. He did not have a fever, yet she felt uncomfortable sending a possibly sick child to school. So she decided to let him stay at home for the day.

The next morning the same thing happened. Again the boy claimed to be ill, and though she did not entirely believe him, the mother allowed him to stay home once again.

On the third morning the boy once again called to his mother and told her that he was sick. This time she did not believe him at all and made him get dressed and go to school. She told him that she thought he was just...

...belling the cat.   or   ...crying, "Wolf!"

From *Fabulous Fables: Using Fables with Children*, published by Good Year Books. Copyright © 1991 Linda K. Garrity.

Culminating Activity Pages

Name: _____   Culminating Activity Page 1

Paper Cup and Sock Puppet

Directions:

Make a hole in a paper or styrofoam cup for the nose. Make sure that you can poke your finger through it.

Make an animal face with construction paper and glue it on the cup. The face can be in one piece like a mask or in parts.

Cut finger holes in the sock for body. Add a tail made from paper or felt.

Folded Paper Puppet

Directions:

1. Cut a strip of paper 12" x 4".

2. Fold in half. Fold each half back.

3. Now the strip has four equal parts. Part 1 is the head. Parts 2 and 3 are the mouth. Part 4 is the body.

Cut face and body parts from construction paper and glue on strip.

From *Fabulous Fables: Using Fables with Children,* published by Good Year Books. Copyright © 1991 Linda K. Garrity.

Culminating Activity Page 1 (continued)

Simple Puppets for Acting Out Fables

Finger puppets

Directions:

Cut a strip of construction paper and tape it around your finger. It is now a tube. Slide it off your finger and decorate it with animal ears, face, tail, etc.

 or

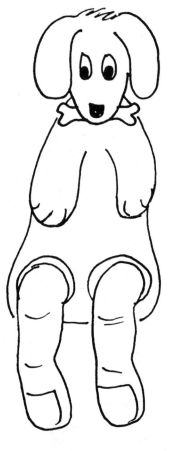

Draw an animal on tagboard and color. Cut out two holes for your fingers. Put your fingers through holes to make the puppet move.

From *Fabulous Fables: Using Fables with Children*, published by Good Year Books. Copyright © 1991 Linda K. Garrity.

Name: _____   **Culminating Activity Page 2**

The Stag and The Hedgehog
by Jackie Moore

Characters: Narrator
            Stag
            Hedgehog
            2 or 3 Deer
            2 or 3 Other Animals
            Goat
            Mrs. Hedgehog
            2 or 3 Other Hedgehogs

Setting: Wheat field

Scene 1: Stag, Hedgehog, some deer and animals. Stag and Hedgehog are watching the animals eat the wheat.

Narrator: A stag and a hedgehog owned a wheat field together. All spring and summer they farmed without a problem. As the wheat began to ripen, they noticed that the other animals were getting into the field and eating the golden grains of ripening wheat.

Deer and Animals: *(eating)* The wheat is delicious!
It will be even better when it's ripe.
Stag and Hedgehog will be angry if they catch us.
Don't worry. Just eat and enjoy!

Stag: *(very angry)* The other animals are eating our wheat!

Hedgehog: At this rate there will not be a grain left by harvest time.

Stag: Those thieving animals have no respect for another's hard work.

Hedgehog: You're bigger than me - you stand guard until harvest time. (Exits.)

Scene 2: Stag and deer are eating wheat, laughing, and talking. Hedgehog is watching from side.

Narrator: At first all went well. Then Hedgehog noticed that the grain was once again being trampled and eaten. He quietly watched one evening and saw Stag greet several other deer and talk, laugh, and eat wheat together.

Deer: *(jumping around)* This is great, Stag, you sure know how to throw a party.

From *Fabulous Fables: Using Fables with Children*, published by Good Year Books. Copyright © 1991 Linda K. Garrity.

Culminating Activity Page 2 (continued)

Stag: Eat up, friends, it's Wheat-er Time! (Everyone jumps up and down laughing)

Narrator: Hedgehog was furious.

Hedgehog: *(goes up to Stag)* A fine guard you make, Stag. Tomorrow I shall take over guarding the field so we can eat next winter.

(All exit.)

Scene 3: Hedgehog marching back and forth. Other animals approach but Hedgehog chases them away.

Narrator: Hedgehog took over the guard. By his very nature he snarled and growled and bristled until the larger animals left the wheatfield. Soon it was Harvest Time.

(Enter Stag.)

Stag: What a lot of wheat we have!

Hedgehog: *(mumbles)* Thanks to me!

Stag: You sure carry a grudge, Hedgehog. Of course, I will need a much larger portion of grain since I am a much larger animal.

Hedgehog: What! If you had kept guarding the field there wouldn't be any wheat to divide. Besides, I might be small but I have a larger family to feed.

Narrator: They argued and argued until a goat came by.

(Enter Goat.)

Stag: Hey Goat. Could you come here and settle an argument?

(Goat approaches Stag and Hedgehog. All huddle together.)

Narrator: Stag and Hedgehog explained their problem.

Goat: *(stepping back)* I have a solution but you both must do as I say.

Stag: Right on!

Hedgehog: You're in charge, Goat!

From *Fabulous Fables: Using Fables with Children*, published by Good Year Books. Copyright © 1991 Linda K. Garrity.

Culminating Activity Page 2 (continued)

Goat: You should run a race with Winner Take All!

Hedgehog: *(jumping up and down)* What! No way! I'm too tiny to race a swift stag like him!

Stag: I'm in! Sounds fine to me.

Hedgehog: Looks like no choice for me. I'm going home to talk to my wife. (Exits.)

Narrator: After Hedgehog stomped away for home, the goat turned to the stag and said:

Goat: I made this decision only because I knew you'll give me part of the wheat if you win. Hedgehog won't do that, he's too honest!

Stag: You're right, Goat. I'll win and I'll give you one-fourth of the grain.

Goat: I'd rather have half, but OK.

Scene 4: Wheat field. Stag is running alone towards finish line.

Narrator: That afternoon Stag and Hedgehog started the race. Stag loped swiftly along the course. He was confident that he would win.

Stag: There's the finish line. I'm going to win.

Mrs. Hedgehog: *(races in front of stag)* Not so fast, Stag. Here I go.

Narrator: Stag was baffled to see the hedgehog scurry over the finish line. (Hedgehog jumps for joy!)

Stag: I can't believe it! You beat me! (Storms off.)

Narrator: Later as Hedgehog and his wife passed out grain to their friends and relatives they looked at each other and chuckled. (All hedgehogs gather together. Mr. and Mrs. Hedgehog step forward.)

Mrs. Hedgehog: Those two crooks think all hedgehogs look alike. I didn't think they would notice if I slipped in and ran the last part of the race.

Hedgehog: You're the Greatest! (Kisses her. Exit together.)

Narrator: The moral of this story: You may need to cheat to deal with cheaters.

From *Fabulous Fables: Using Fables with Children*, published by Good Year Books. Copyright © 1991 Linda K. Garrity.

Name: _____ **Culminating Activity Page 3**

Animal Patterns

From *Fabulous Fables: Using Fables with Children,* published by Good Year Books. Copyright © 1991 Linda K. Garrity.

Culminating Activity Page 3 (continued)

From *Fabulous Fables: Using Fables with Children*, published by Good Year Books. Copyright © 1991 Linda K. Garrity.

Culminating Activity Page 3 (continued)

Crocodile

Bear

From *Fabulous Fables: Using Fables with Children*, published by Good Year Books. Copyright © 1991 Linda K. Garrity.

Culminating Activity Page 3 (continued)

Stork

Dog

From *Fabulous Fables: Using Fables with Children*, published by Good Year Books. Copyright © 1991 Linda K. Garrity.

Culminating Activity Page 3 (continued)

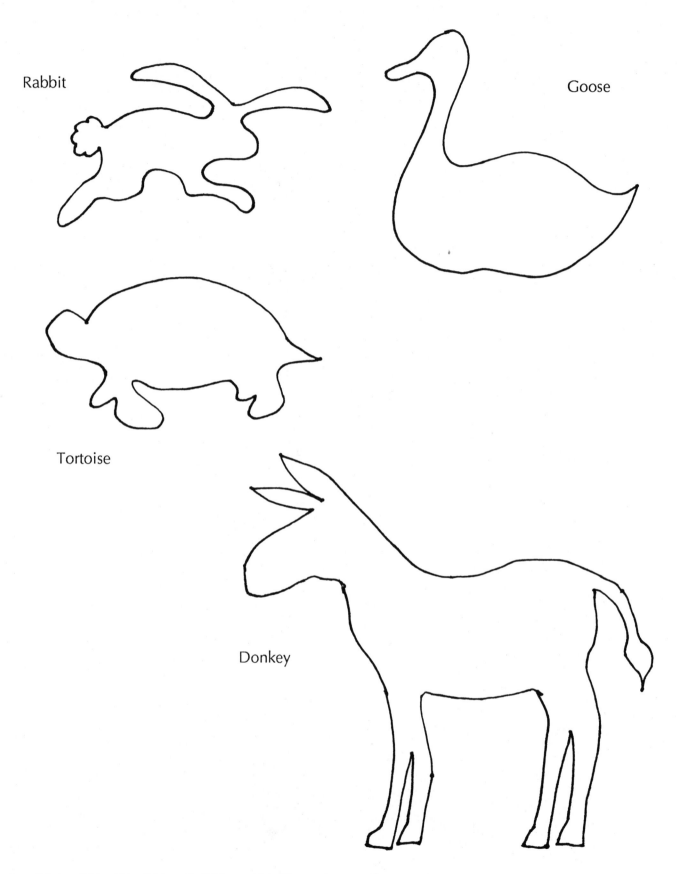

Culminating Activity Page 3 (continued)

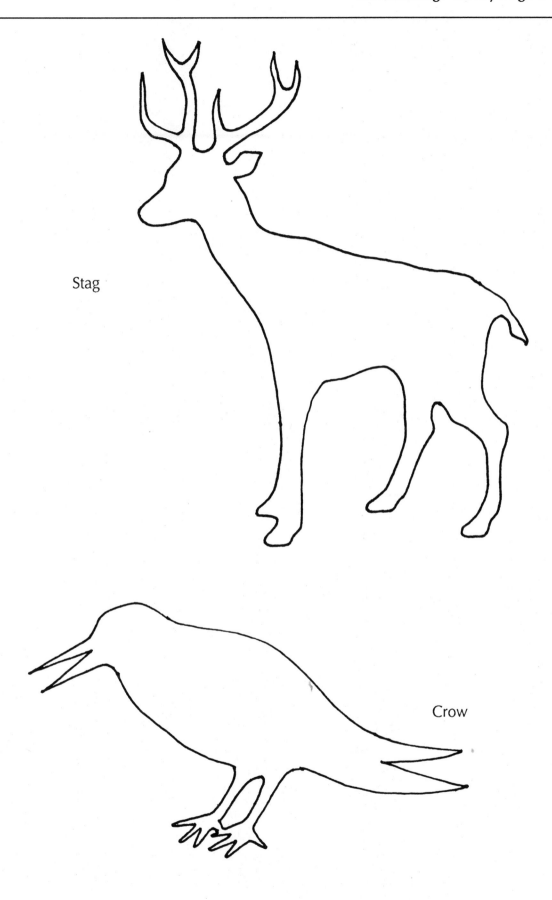

Name: _____   Culminating Activity Page 4

Four Simple Character Mobiles

Directions:

Draw and color pictures or use animal patterns for the parts of the mobile.
Print the title on one piece of the mobile, and print the moral on the back of the title.

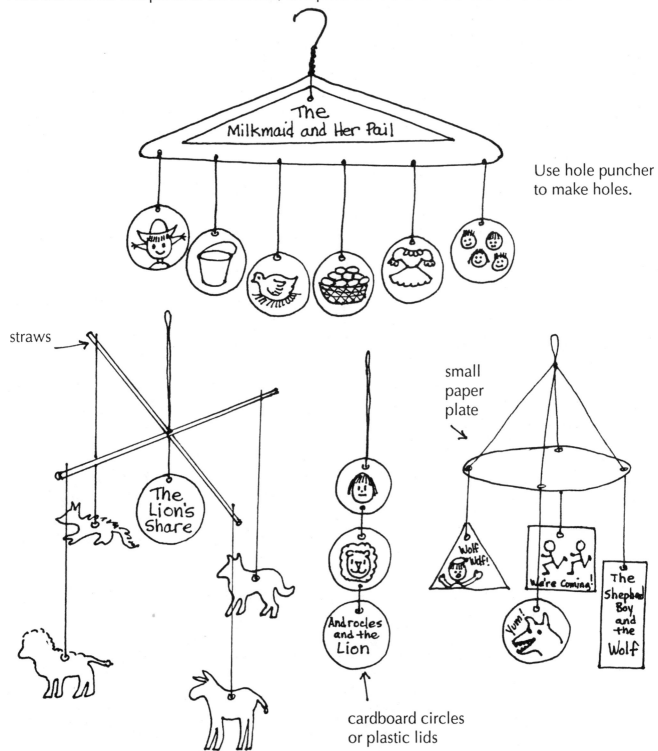

Use hole puncher to make holes.

straws

small paper plate

cardboard circles or plastic lids

From *Fabulous Fables: Using Fables with Children*, published by Good Year Books. Copyright © 1991 Linda K. Garrity.

Name: _____   **Culminating Activity Page 5**

Directions:

Cut out the cards. See if a friend can name the title of each fable. Make two copies of each card, turn them over and play Memory (matching pairs).

From *Fabulous Fables: Using Fables with Children*, published by Good Year Books. Copyright © 1991 Linda K. Garrity.

Culminating Activity Page 5 (continued)

From *Fabulous Fables: Using Fables with Children*, published by Good Year Books. Copyright © 1991 Linda K. Garrity.

Name: _____

Culminating Activity Page 6

Directions:
Listed below are 20 of the animals most often found in fables. Find them in the word search.

Hare	Lion	Wolf	Stork
Tortoise	Mouse	Donkey	Monkey
Stag	Ant	Goat	Crocodile
Hedgehog	Dove	Dog	Bear
Crow	Fox	Goose	Deer

```
M O N K E T X O G H S T A D
O C W C R O W G O A T O H E
N R O X F R A C D R O X E E
K O L B E T N R E G R B D E
E C M G S O T O L I K E X L
Y L F O R I X C A N M O U I
S X M O U S E E H E D G O D
T C H A R E V M O N B H E O
O R E E D O M O X R V E V C
R S T O D O N K E Y S T A O
C T O B E G O O S E D X B R
R G O O D E E R L X G O R C
A N M E I G T H I T U N E R
N I G X B U R W O L F L W O
D E M O U S L I N G H A R C
```

The words may go up, down, or diagonal.

From *Fabulous Fables: Using Fables with Children*, published by Good Year Books. Copyright © 1991 Linda K. Garrity.

Name: _____   Culminating Activity Page 7

Fables Story Report

Title of Fable: _____
Explain what you learned from this fable:
_____
_____
_____
_____
_____

Directions:
Draw in the main characters' faces. You can make finger puppets for fable plays when you take the report home.

Name: _____   Name: _____   Name: _____

From *Fabulous Fables: Using Fables with Children*, published by Good Year Books. Copyright © 1991 Linda K. Garrity.

Bibliography

Fable Collections

Aesop. *The Aesop for Children,* illus. by Milo Winter. Rand McNally & Co., 1984. First published in 1919.

This reprint of the 1919 edition is an excellent selection for a comprehensive volume of Aesop. It includes 126 fables along with an abundant number of Milo Winter's original color illustrations. The only drawback to this collection is its lack of index.

Aesop. *Aesop's Fables,* illus. by Michael Hague. Holt, Rinehart and Winston, 1985.

Michael Hague's lovely paintings of anthropomorphic animals bear a decidedly old English flair. This well-designed book contains thirteen of the most familiar fables, and each includes a full-page painting. This is a good choice for children to use individually, as they need to be close to the illustrations to appreciate their detail. Children may not catch all of the drollery of the setting and costumes, but they will certainly enjoy the book and understand that fables are old, imaginary animal stories.

Aesop. *Aesop's Fables,* illus. by Heidi Holder. Viking Press, 1981.

A full-page, beautifully detailed watercolor painting accompanies each of the nine fables in this collection. Heidi Holder has selected a medieval theme, complete with intricate borders and illuminated first letters. This is an excellent collection for older children to read to themselves and pore over the pen-and-ink and watercolor artwork.

Aesop. *The Caldecott Aesop,* illus. by Randolph Caldecott. Doubleday, 1978. First published in 1883.

This reprint is an important addition to children's literature because it preserves the outstanding drawings of Randolph Caldecott, a pioneer in children's book illustrations and the namesake of the prestigious Caldecott Award. Twenty fables, some popular and some virtually unknown, have been reprinted here with the drawings touched up with modern watercolor techniques. Following each fable is a drawing showing Caldecott's interpretation of a modern application of the moral. Of course, "modern" in this case means what was considered modern in 1883, the original publication date. These additions are interesting but will be difficult for most children to understand.

Alley, R. W. *Seven Fables from Aesop,* illus. by R. W. Alley. Dodd, Mead & Company, 1986.

Seven of the most famous fables are retold simply and illustrated charmingly with soft watercolors in this collection for children in the primary grades.

Anno, Mitsumasa. *Anno's Aesop,* illus. by Mitsumasa Anno. Orchard Books, 1987.

Published in the United States in 1989, *Anno's Aesop* is a welcome newcomer to the field. Anno, a distinguished author/illustrator known for his imaginative picture books, has used a traditional translation for the fables but has added a running commentary, based solely upon the illustrations, across the bottom of the pages. The commentary shows that the stories can be viewed in more than one way, particularly if one doesn't read the text. The book contains forty-one fables and can be used easily without the commentary. Lively illustrations, an interesting explanation of the origin of the fables, and a table of contents make this new entry a good quality addition to a fable collection.

From *Fabulous Fables: Using Fables with Children,* published by Good Year Books. Copyright © 1991 Linda K. Garrity.

Carle, Eric. *Eric Carle's Treasury of Classic Stories for Children,* illus. by Eric Carle. Orchard Books, 1988.

This anthology contains tales by the Brothers Grimm and Hans Christian Andersen, plus the Aesop's fables featured in Carle's own *Twelve Tales from Aesop*. The additional folklore in this volume, which children always enjoy, make it a good purchase for home use.

Carle, Eric. *Fairy Tales and Fables,* ed. by Eve Morel, illus. by Gyo Fujikawa. Grosset & Dunlap, 1982.

This trade edition contains ten fables as well as an assortment of well-known folktales. This is an inexpensive storybook appropriate for home use.

Carle, Eric. *Twelve Tales from Aesop,* illus. by Eric Carle. Philomel Books, 1980.

Brightly illustrated with Carle's distinctive collage-type artwork, this handsome book will appeal especially to younger children. The full-page pictures with whimsical animals and the smooth retellings make the book appropriate for large group presentation as well as individual enjoyment.

Galdone, Paul. *Three Aesop Fox Fables,* illus. by Paul Galdone. Seabury Press, 1971.

Galdone selected "The Fox and the Grapes," "The Fox and the Stork," and "The Fox and the Crow" to retell and illustrate in his inimitable style. The large expressive illustrations of animals make this an excellent choice for a group presentation. This book is representative of Galdone's outstanding work in folk literature.

Jacobs, Joseph. *The Fables of Aesop,* illus. by Richard Heighway. Schocken Books, 1966. First published in 1894. Available in paperback.

Joseph Jacobs first retold and printed this extensive collection of fables in 1894. Written and illustrated in an old English style, the book offers a contrast to modern versions.

Lewis, Naomi. *Cry Wolf and Other Aesop Fables,* illus. by Barry Castle. Oxford University Press, 1988.

Naomi Lewis' rendition of Aesop is unusual, with succinct fables that seem closer to the original style than most. The morals are explained in poetry form (rhyming couplets) and offer comment on the story while pointing out the moral truth. The paintings by Barry Castle are exquisite. The style of the fables, artwork, and poetic commentaries would make this book more appropriate for older children.

Mathias, Robert. *Aesop's Fables,* color illustrations by David Frankland, line illustrations by Meg Rutherford. Silver Burdett, 1986.

A well-written and attractively designed book containing fifty-nine fables, this volume would serve as a good basic purchase for a fable collection.

Paxton, Tom. *Aesop's Fables,* illus. by Robert Rayevsky. Morrow & Co., 1988.

Outstanding illustrations set against an authentic medieval background mark this new collection of ten fables. Tom Paxton has retold the fables in lyrical verse that almost begs to be sung aloud. This fine book should be used along with the more traditional fable forms to highlight the creativity of this style.

Reeves, James. *Fables from Aesop,* illus. by Maurice Wilson. P. Bedrick Books, 1962.

This is an excellent version to use with younger children because the narrative has been expanded and enlivened with bright dialogue. The watercolor illustrations, about half of which are in color, are appealing. In addition, there is an index, a handy tool in a large fable anthology.

Testa, Fulvio. *Aesop's Fables,* illus. by Fulvio Testa. Barron's, 1989.

Fulvio Testa, an Italian picture book illustrator and author, has created this new collection of

From *Fabulous Fables: Using Fables with Children,* published by Good Year Books. Copyright © 1991 Linda K. Garrity.

twenty fables. The fables are brief, staying close to the traditional text, though the morals are implied, not stated separately. Each fable has an outstanding, full-page watercolor picture. Most of the fables in this book are lesser known here in America. That fact, along with the artwork and the clear, interesting writing style, make this an important purchase for a fable collection.

Watson, Carol. *Aesop's Fables,* illus. by Nick Price. Usborne Publishing, 1982. Available in paperback.
   Carol Watson retells ten of the most familiar fables in a simplified, cartoon-style version designed for children to read to themselves. Also available in an inexpensive paperback binding, this is an attractive "additional" book for a fable collection.

Single Fables from Aesop

Aesop. *The Miller, His Son, and Their Donkey,* illus. by Eugen Sopko. North-South Books, 1984.
   This is a lovely picture book, illustrated with full-page layouts and soft, warm colors. The text is spare and typeset with large bold print. The book is both an excellent choice for group presentation and for younger children to read to themselves.

Castle, Caroline. *The Hare and the Tortoise,* illus. by Peter Weevers. Dutton, 1985.
   Caroline Castle has expanded this fable into a more lengthy story. Dressed in turn-of-the-century costumes, the animals assume more detailed characterization. Children will greatly enjoy this embellished version.

Cauley, Lorinda Bryan. *The Town Mouse and the Country Mouse,* illus. by Lorinda Bryan Cauley. Putnam, 1984.
   This is an outstanding rendition of the fable of the two mouse cousins. The expanded story line and rich, colorful illustrations set in the Victorian era make this book a fine addition to a fable collection.

Galdone, Paul. *The Hare and the Tortoise,* illus. by Paul Galdone. McGraw-Hill, 1962.
   Large, expressive illustrations of animals fill the pages of this good quality version, which has not been expanded extensively. The large print and straightforward language make this a good version for children to read to themselves.

Patterson, Geoffrey. *The Goose that Laid the Golden Egg,* illus. by Geoffrey Patterson. Andre Deutsch, 1986.
   Geoffrey Patterson retells this old folktale-fable with a European flair in a creative picture book format. Using heavy brown paper for the background, the artist sketched with pen and ink, adding small amounts of rich color for highlighting. As an added touch, the eggs are a metallic gold. This cozy, charming book is only sold in a trade binding.

Roach, Marilynne K. *Two Roman Mice,* illus. by Marilynne Roach. Crowell, 1975.
   In addition to translating "The Town Mouse and the Country Mouse" from its original Latin, and retelling the story, Marilynne Roach has illustrated this small book with black and white drawings with an authentic ancient Roman setting. This is a good selection for contrasting single volumes of this tale.

Stevens, Janet. *Androcles and the Lion,* illus. by Janet Stevens. Holiday House, 1989.
   Younger children will enjoy this colorful, somewhat sentimentalized version of the fable. Catherine Storr's book on the same fable has more depth and gives more detail of early Roman life, though Stevens' version, with the engaging animals, may be more appropriate for early primary children.

From *Fabulous Fables: Using Fables with Children,* published by Good Year Books. Copyright © 1991 Linda K. Garrity.

Stevens, Janet. *The Tortoise and the Hare,* illus. by Janet Stevens. Holiday House, 1984.

Expanded into a picture book, Stevens' colorful updated version of "The Tortoise and the Hare" is a fine choice for young children.

Stevens, Janet. *The Town Mouse and the Country Mouse,* illus. by Janet Stevens. Holiday House, 1987.

Huge, bold illustrations fill the pages of this expanded fable. Set in modern times, this version, like Cauley's fine book, is a recommended purchase, although this book would work well with a slightly younger audience than Cauley's book.

Storr, Catherine. *Androcles and the Lion,* illus. by Philip Hood. Raintree Publishers, 1986.

Storr's book expands this fable into an engrossing, full-length picture book. The story adds many historical details on the life of slaves during the days of the Roman Empire. Large, colorful pictures help make this story exciting and understandable for most age groups.

Wildsmith, Brian. *The Miller, the Boy and the Donkey.* Franklin Watts, 1969.

Based on La Fontaine's fable, this version is succinctly told and beautifully illustrated with bright watercolors and geometric patterns. The book is one of the older individual fables still in print, and fortunately so, as Wildsmith's work is timeless.

Wildsmith, Brian. *The Rich Man and the Shoemaker.* Franklin Watts, 1979.

Wildsmith's rendition of this La Fontaine fable is done as well as the above-mentioned book. Two other single-fable picture books printed at about the same time, *The North Wind and the Sun* and *The Lion and the Rat,* are now out of print. Many libraries with slightly older collections will be able to supply these additional titles to Wildsmith's fine foursome.

Fables from Other Cultures

Bierhorst, John. *Doctor Coyote: A Native American's Aesop's Fables,* illus. by Wendy Watson. Macmillan, 1987.

Doctor Coyote is a unique, outstanding collection of fables. Based on a copy of Aesop that was translated into the Aztec language in the sixteenth century, Bierhorst's retelling fully captures the spirit of both Aesop and the Native Americans' coyote-trickster tales. Further enriching the text is Wendy Watson's clever, colorful illustrations with their humorous animal characters and authentic New Mexican setting. Older children will be challenged to match the analogous tales from traditional Aesop collections to these tales. They might also like to study further the Native American trickster tales. Younger children will be content merely to enjoy the delightful stories and pictures.

Brown, Marcia. *Once a Mouse,* illus. by Marcia Brown. Scribner's, 1961. Available in paperback.

This ancient fable from the Indian Hitopadesa brought Marcia Brown a Caldecott Award for the outstanding woodcut illustrations. Still in print and now available in paperback, this is a basic purchase for any fable library collection.

Demi. *A Chinese Zoo.* Harcourt Brace Jovanovich, 1987.

Demi has selected thirteen ancient Chinese fables to retell and illustrate in a most unique style. This large picture book features a single fable on each two-page spread with the narrative divided evenly between the two pages. A large fan covered with the animal characters fills the two pages; the moral is written beneath the fan in both English and Chinese characters. The background of each two-page spread is a vivid solid color, with the color fading almost to white at the binding. Though some of these fables date back to 7000 B.C., it is interesting to note that they sound familiar and probably were antedated by Indian fables from an even earlier time. This is an outstanding book, beautifully and thoughtfully created.

From *Fabulous Fables: Using Fables with Children,* published by Good Year Books. Copyright © 1991 Linda K. Garrity.

Demi. *Demi's Reflective Fables.* Grosset & Dunlap, 1988.

    Demi's latest Chinese fable collection is a marvelous creation. Inspired by ancient Chinese mirrors, Demi illustrated each of the thirteen stories with a large round painting. Each fable is typeset in a circular pattern with a colorful border around it. The "reflective" aspect of the book refers to the mirror-like design and the contemplative nature of the fables. This book is aimed at an older audience than *A Chinese Zoo.*

Galdone, Paul. *The Monkey and the Crocodile.* Clarion Books, 1969. Available in paperback.

    Paul Galdone's talent for drawing large, expressive animals with yellow eyes is put to a good use in this ancient Jataka tale from India. That toothsome crocodile and wily monkey almost leap across the page as they try to outsmart one another. Sadly, this talented man is no longer with us to bring the pleasure of folk literature to children.

Galdone, Paul. *The Turtle and the Monkey,* illus. by Paul Galdone. Clarion Books, 1983.

    In this episodic fable from the Philippines, the self-centered monkey and the clever turtle try to outwit one another, with the turtle having the final victory in a "Brer Rabbit"-type ending. This is an engrossing tale painted in the rich watercolors of the Philippine jungle.

Ivanov, Anatoly. *Ol' Jake's Lucky Day,* illus. by Anatoly Ivanov. Lothrop, Lee & Shepard, 1984.

    Ivanov has captured the old Russian fable with vigor and authenticity in this colorful picture book, an amusing book for all ages.

Kamen, Gloria. *The Ringdoves,* illus. by Gloria Kamen. Atheneum, 1988.

    A beautifully illustrated and retold rendition of a single fable of Bidpai, this is one of the few outstanding Indian fable books available in America. The rich artwork uses the colors and designs of ancient India. This is a fine book that will appeal to any age.

Plante, Patricia, and David Bergman. *The Turtle and Two Ducks: Animal Fables Retold from La Fontaine,* illus. by Anne Rockwell. Crowell, 1981.

    This book contains eleven of La Fontaine's fables, retold and illustrated in a lighthearted style, complete with seventeenth-century French costumes and tiny animated creatures. These stories and pictures are appealing to younger children, who delight in the lively, miniscule drawings.

Modern Fables and Fable Parodies

Lionni, Leo. *Frederick's Fables,* illus. by Leo Lionni. Pantheon Books, 1985.

    Considered one of the finest creators of modern fables for children, Lionni has assembled thirteen of his previously published picture books into one large volume. Lionni's brilliant collage-type illustrations help to make this an outstanding purchase and a good comparison to the animal fable collections from the past.

Lobel, Arnold. *Fables,* illus. by Arnold Lobel. Harper & Row, 1980. Available in paperback.

    Lobel won the Newbery Award for this book of twenty original fables, each illustrated with a full-page painting. These amusing fables and droll illustrations reveal Lobel's well-honed sense of humor. A delight for any age!

McFarland, John. *The Exploding Frog and Other Fables from Aesop,* illus. by James Marshall. Little, Brown, 1981. Available in paperback.

    James Marshall's illustrations will seem familiar to children who have grown up on his delightful books. This edition contains thirty-six fables, which stick fairly close to Aesop (a lighter tone and humorous lines have been added). The illustrations are what truly add the humor. Children will love hearing these fables as well as reading the book to themselves.

From Fabulous Fables: Using Fables with Children, *published by Good Year Books. Copyright © 1991 Linda K. Garrity.*

Miller, Edna. *Mousekin's Fables,* illus. by Edna Miller. Prentice Hall, 1982.

Aesop's fables were the basis for these original stories about woodland creatures. Each month features a different story, ending in a traditional proverb. Soft watercolors fill the pages. Though this is an attractive book, most children will prefer the original Aesop to this version.

Ross, Tony. *The Boy Who Cried Wolf,* illus. by Tony Ross. Dial Books, 1985.

Ross' zany illustrations of the debonair wolf create a wickedly funny version of this old fable. The twisted ending keeps the reader guessing right up to the last page.

Ross, Tony. *Foxy Fables,* illus. by Tony Ross. Dial Books, 1986.

This hilarious parody of Aesop features six fables. The comic, exuberant illustrations are a perfect accompaniment to this refreshing book, which will appeal especially to older children.

Index to Fables

Androcles and the Lion, 42
The Ant and the Dove, 42
The Ant and the Grasshopper, 54
The Boy and His Mother (Garrity), 60
The Boy Who Cried Wolf, 53
The Bundle of Sticks, 50
The Crow and the Pitcher, 41
The Dog and His Shadow, 45
The Dog in the Manger, 48
The Donkey in the Lion's Skin (Indian Jataka tale), 55
The Elephant and the Carpenters (Indian Jataka tale), 58
The Farmer and the Hare (Russian), 47
The Fox and the Grapes, 51
The Fox and the Sick Lion, 49
The Fox and the Stork, 48
The Golden Goose (Indian Jataka tale), 57
The Goose that Laid the Golden Egg, 45
The Hare and the Rumor (Indian Jataka tale), 56
The Hermit and the Mouse (Indian Hitopadesa tale), 54
The Lion and the Mouse, 41
The Lion, the Wolf, and the Fox, 49
The Lion's Share, 44
Lunch (Garrity), 60
The Milkmaid and Her Pail, 47
The Monkey and the Crocodile (Indian Jataka tale), 52
The Report Card (Garrity), 59
The Stag and the Hedgehog, 39
The Tortoise and the Hare, 39
The Town Mouse and the Country Mouse, 46
The Two Travellers and the Bear, 51
The Wind and The Sun, 43
A Wolf in Sheep's Clothing, 52

From *Fabulous Fables: Using Fables with Children,* published by Good Year Books. Copyright © 1991 Linda K. Garrity.